Nobody seems to know for certain what a cat is or where it came from, though everyone has a theory.

Pliny tells us that some six hundred years before the Prophet, Arabs worshiped a golden cat and believed that there was such special cleanliness and purity about cats that their origin must have been distinct from that of ordinary creatures. . . .

In classical mythology Apollo created the lion to scare his sister Diana, and to tease him she mocked his invention by creating the cat.

In the West of Ireland they say that at some turning point in the world's history the snakes turned into cats, which is why the cat's bite is venomous. . . .

The first famous cats were Egyptian, which proves only that imperial gods leave records that endure for five thousand years and house pets don't.

Also by Barbara Holland:

ONE'S COMPANY*
HAIL TO THE CHIEFS*
MOTHER'S DAY, OR THE VIEW FROM IN HERE

Published by Ballantine Books

SECRETS OF THE CAT:
ITS LORE, LEGEND, AND LIVES

(Formerly titled *The Name of the Cat*)

Barbara Holland
Illustrations by Emily Schilling

IVY BOOKS • NEW YORK

Ivy Books
Published by Ballantine Books
Copyright © 1988 by Barbara Holland

All rights reserved under International and Pan-American Copyright Conventions. Published in the United States by Ballantine Books, a division of Random House, Inc., New York, and distributed in Canada by Random House of Canada Limited, Toronto. Originally published under the title *The Name of the Cat* by Dodd, Mead & Company, Inc. in 1988.

Library of Congress Catalog Card Number: 88-92245

ISBN 0-8041-1276-2

Printed in Canada

First Ballantine Books Trade Edition: June 1989
First Ballantine Books Mass Market Edition: July 1994

10 9 8 7 6 5

Cover photo © Walter Chandoha

To Sidney

Contents

1

The Conversion of Boston Blackie

You can usually tell by looking at it what's going on inside a dog. Except for the few Thurberian neurotics, a dog wears his insides on his outside, writ large and plain. A cat thinks at the back of its head, and the results can surprise you. No wonder cats were burned as witches; it hurts people's feelings not to know what the lower orders are up to.

Boston Blackie was an outlaw. He was of the tribe known in the city as alley cats, in the country as feral, and in the suburbs as strays, the last word carrying a hint of self-righteous blame; to stray is to wander, ignorantly or willfully, from the proper path. It is the cat who has gone astray, wandered off from domesticity to starve, not the people who have left it behind when they moved or thrown it in a bag with its siblings from a passing car. There are millions of these. They flicker across human paths from time to time, and maybe we say, "Puss, puss," but they vanish as quickly as the shadow of a bird, having no reason to answer. They do not live long, but there are always more.

Boston Blackie was different from most. He was more predator than waif, and his chosen prey was cats. Boston Blackie hated cats; he wanted to kill them, all of them. Coming down out of the woods and fields like the wolf on

1

the fold, he swooped, savaged, and vanished again. My sister Judy and her husband had, at the time, thirteen cats (they now have twenty-three, through no fault of their own) and, weather permitting, these spent most of their time outdoors. Boston Blackie attacked them on their own premises without regard for age or gender, and he beat them bloody. He ripped their ears and gouged their eyes and dealt out deep, suppurating abscesses. Cat after cat was carried bleeding to the vet, cat after cat was dosed with penicillin. Yards of stitches were taken. The vet bills grew.

Sometimes we caught glimpses of Blackie; sometimes we just heard screams. His attack was most uncatlike, with none of the singsong preliminaries to a fight, no foreplay, none of the elaborate adjustment of position and subtleties of eye contact with which normal male cats defuse their aggressions, nine times out of ten breaking off to lick or pretend an interest in some distant object and drift away without a blow exchanged. Blackie just pounced, as on a mouse. Anyone around would run out yelling. Once I beat him with a rake, standing over him panting and whacking, but he went on tearing chunks out of poor Flanagan as if I were made of air. He had no interest in people. I was unnerved by the single-minded concentration of his hatred, like the legends about wolverines. Nothing distracted him from his urge to rid the world of all its other cats; when disturbed by humans he usually drove his victim under the woodshed, out of reach, to go on with the bloodshed. Not even the largest and strongest of our cats landed a blow, and Blackie himself was unscarred. Cats fight by certain rules and ceremonies, and Blackie's bulletlike descent and mad, meaningless hatred disarmed them utterly; they never even had a chance to run. Some of their wounds were on their back legs from trying.

Except for a handful accidentally born on the premises, all Judy's cats had been strays, and none of them had ever acted like that. Stray cats may be, and usually are, starving, lame, frightened, ill, and in hideous pain from infected wounds, eaten alive by fleas, ticks, ear mites, and intestinal parasites, but they don't go looking for other cats to kill. Since the thirteen had all been neutered, sex could be ruled out as a motive, and Blackie wasn't starving, either. When Judy fed her own she threw a propitiatory handful of food into the forsythia bushes where he often lay in wait, not for food but for blood.

He didn't act like a cat, and he didn't even look much like a stray. The standard homeless cat is a brindled mix of stripes and patches, leggy, with a long nose and close-set eyes and an overall look of skimpiness, as if there hadn't been enough protoplasm to create him properly. Basic out-laws are slat-sided, and almost disappear when seen from above; Blackie was square. He was short of leg and round of ear, with immensely long white whiskers and very small white feet, an outlaw of a different breed.

Conferences were held.

"He's insane," we said. "He's psychotic."

"At least he can't be rabid. He's been coming around for months, since the middle of winter, and if he had rabies he'd be long dead."

"If only the other cats would stick together. Gang up on him."

"Cats don't join armies."

"Besides, they're all afraid of him. It's like saying, why didn't the plane passengers gang up on the hijackers? Who's going to gang up first?"

"If we could just get hold of him somehow and take him to the SPCA."

"You're not suggesting we pick him up? In our *hands*?"

"Maybe if we could catch him in one of those box traps, and then just leave him in the trap and put it in the car?"

The vet, who was sympathetic to our efforts and bored with cleaning and stitching up wounds, lent us a drop-gate trap and offered to kill the madman if we caught him. Blackie avoided the trap. It can't have been very convinc-ing; no matter what we baited it with, nothing at all went into it.

Blackie ambushed the smallest and prettiest of the Three Girls and ripped her ear and slashed her eye.

"We could poison him," said Judy. "I throw food into the bushes for him. I could poison it."

"That would be the day he was off killing someone else's cats. One of ours would find it instead."

"We could shoot him."

It kept coming around to that. At first it was a joke. We weren't people with guns, and God knows we weren't people who shot cats. Shot *cats*? Judy and Bob were a famous hostel for needy cats, and bore, they always said, an invisible mark on the door such as bums were said to make during the Great Depression, meaning "Here are softies." But summer came, and Blackie's terrorist attacks continued; no cat had actually been killed yet, but antibiotic pills had become a time-consuming part of the family routine, and the gun came to seem less bizarre.

"He's probably in some kind of pain," we argued. "That could be why he's so vicious. It would be a mercy to shoot him."

"He might have had a head injury. Something pressing on his brain makes him berserk."

"Where would we get this gun?"

"Terry's got one. He's got a whole armory, actually, but he could bring something lightweight that wouldn't knock holes in the neighborhood."

"Would he do it for us?"

"Sure. We'll give him a beer. I don't suppose it'll be the first cat he's shot; he's one of those sportsmen types."

"After all, we have to think of our own. They can't live like this."

"It's agreed, then."

We had sat in judgment on Blackie and pronounced him miserable, in pain as well as psychotic. Besides, we wouldn't have to pull the trigger personally, just point out the lurking Blackie and go inside and hold our ears, praying that Terry, not a cat person, could tell one black cat with white trim from the others.

"We're going away for the weekend," said Judy. "We'll be back Tuesday. Let's do it Tuesday night at feeding time."

"Tuesday night." We all nodded, feeling that we should prick our fingers and seal the decision in blood, to share the guilt equally.

Judy and Bob went away for the weekend, and I fed their cats. Feeding their cats was not child's play. The assortment of battered tins and dishes covered half the backyard, and protocol had to be observed. Muffie, senior cat and major-domo and sergeant-at-arms, followed me into the kitchen to supervise. It was one of his duties to see that meals were served on time, and to find and chivvy the feeder if they were late. Muffie was getting old, but he delegated no responsibility, had no lieutenants, and no other cat seemed ready to take over and let him retire. He was looking a bit careworn and heavy in his mind. Poor Muff, he would have loved more frequent laps, or a word of appreciation, but in households so crowded the attention goes more often than it should to the young, the cute, and the pushy.

I dumped a large can of cat food into a kettle of dry chows, poured water over it, and mashed and stirred the mess vigorously while Muffie watched and the others took up their stations on the lawn.

Zachary was fed on the back step, and first; at the time, Judy still considered him the baby of the family, though she's had an accident since that wiped out his title. He is a curious-looking cat. His sharply crossed eyes are Siamese-blue and his body is buff, but his legs and tail are striped. Judy loyally insists that he's a tabby-point Siamese, a recognized creature in English show circles, but nothing about his shape or voice suggests Siam. Was he the product of a misalliance, or the result of some misguided breeding experiment? Apparently his owners had been dissatisfied with him and cut off his whiskers and threw him away in a patch of steep, rocky woods; he was too small to have wandered so far from human habitation on his own, half starved and screaming lonesomely to himself when Judy found him.

The Three Girls—Stubby, Gray, and beautiful Marzipan—eat together out of one rusty pan, and care must be taken that their mother, Mehitabel the witch, doesn't chase them away from it; she never could stand them, even when they were tiny. She was found, pregnant, in a dumpster at a construction site, and Judy and Bob often said, "You can take the cat out of the dumpster, but you can't take the dumpster out of the cat."

Throw a handful at the bushes for Blackie. Like throwing salt over your shoulder to ward off evil spirits.

Ferdy, whose teeth are bad, eats last and gets the softened juicy dregs at the bottom of the kettle. I never come out quite even and have to hustle around snatching back some from the other dishes, but when you've finished feeding Judy's cats you've accomplished something, and can stand back and survey the seething lawn with pride.

I had gotten as far as, I think, Porky, when Boston Blackie came out of the bushes.

The other cats froze, and then the ones closest to the woods began to slip away. Marzipan broke and ran, like a fool, followed by her sisters, and Muffie edged backwards toward the kitchen door. I stood still.

Where had Judy left the cat carrier, in case someone had to be rushed to the vet? Why hadn't we called Terry at once, on Thursday, as soon as we decided on the gun? Could I call him now? Would he get here in time?

Blackie walked steadily across the grass toward me, and I backed against a tree. I had never heard of a cat walking up to a human and attacking it, but I've learned to be wary of generalizations about cats, and this was no common cat.

He moved purposefully, without haste, and ignored the other cats melting away, ignored their abandoned dishes.

In front of me he stopped and looked up, and I looked down, hugging the kettle as a kind of bulletproof vest. His tail was high in the classic greeting gesture. He opened his mouth and gave a ridiculously small hoarse mew.

It was the first time he had ever noticed any of us. It was absurd to think of it, but could it be a trick? A trap? "Are you hungry, Blackie?" I asked in nervous falsetto. "Help yourself. The others lost their appetites." I could reach down and grab him, if only I had steel gloves on. Throw him loose in the car and drive hell-for-leather to the SPCA's gas chamber.

He lifted a front paw and curled it, and mewed again.

"You mean you want a plate of your *own*?" I asked.

Apparently he did. I went and got one, and filled it, and he settled quietly to his dinner without glancing around, tail down and stretched out in the classic gesture of satisfied dining. One by one the others crept back to gulp a few bites from their own plates, never taking their eyes off the guest, but he paid no attention. He ate daintily and slowly, and when he was finished he washed his white paws and whiskers and then went over to the daylily bed against the sunny wall and found a patch that hadn't already been marked off by other cats and stretched out and closed his eyes, crushing daylilies.

He's called Basil now, and sometimes Bison because his head and shoulders have grown to enormous size, and he purrs like a helicopter. He's been known to cuff an unruly kitten, but otherwise peace is his whole desire, peace and for pure heaven a little rubbing under the chin until his purr amplifies to the gurgle of a Boeing with a sea gull in its throat.

I have coaxed wild cats in from the woods before, and this is not how it's done. It's a long process and full of set-backs. First the dish at the edge of the lawn is ignored completely or falls to a raccoon. Then the food is eaten, but secretly, at night. Then if all goes well and no one slams a door, no far-off dog barks, no phone rings, maybe there's a glimpse of cat at the dish at dusk. Emboldened, you move the dish six feet in from the woods, onto civilized grass, where it stays untouched for three days. You may never see the cat again, or it may eventually reappear to snatch a morsel and race with it back to the woods.

With Rupert, I began in July, and by the time leaves were falling in October he would suffer me to sit on the back steps and watch him eating from twenty feet away. After that I had to go away and my mother took over. By first snowfall she had him in the house, but now after twelve years of domestic life he's still twitchy about it. He still disappears for hours at the sound of a strange voice. He accepts food from no one but Mother. Two years ago he took to sitting beside her on the couch in the evenings; if he lives long enough he may someday sit in her lap, but he's still terrified of my brother. More than once he's mistaken me for Mother, and when he realized I wasn't, squawled with horror and fled.

Rupert was coaxed with infinite gentleness for months; Boston Blackie, who had known only shouts and occasional beatings from us, converted himself between morning and evening.

What happened? We argued it over. Dr. Jekyll and Mr. Hyde? But there had been no Jekyll moments in his outlaw days, and months passed and Mr. Hyde never returned.

Sometimes desperate circumstance will force a feral cat to ask for help that it hates. Once, in the country, a nursing female came to my back door in bitter January and asked for food. I don't know how she knew to ask, but certainly she knew she had to have help or she and the kittens would die; it's unwise, when you're on your own, to have kittens in zero-degree weather. There was something terribly proud and bitter in this little cat, who didn't pretend to be friendly but only showed me her desperation, her hat-rack hipbones and dry, dangling teats. I put out food and water, and then followed her to the kittens, in the semi-shelter under a shed. They were very young, with their eyes still sealed shut. The little cat growled at me when I reached out a hand, and scratched me when I tried to gather her young up to take them someplace warmer. She had hated having to ask for food, and as soon as a break came in the steely cold she and the surviving kittens disappeared.

But Boston Blackie wasn't hungry, and to a cat who'd

survived the long Pennsylvania winter these June days with their meadows full of mice must have seemed very endurable indeed. People who extol the independent, solitary nature of the cat would have considered his life ideal.

Maybe he had had a spell of madness, or perhaps amnesia. Maybe, since there was a respectable strain of protoplasm in his shape, some racial memory had risen in his brain like a bubble. Maybe he had once belonged to people, and been a house cat, and then lost his sanity or his memory and somehow that Saturday it came back to him. "Maybe," Judy suggested, "he'd had a blow on the head, and then he had another blow on the head and it brought back his memory."

"Like in the cartoons."

"Exactly."

It was a silly idea, but it was the only one we could think of, or the only one we could admit to without making fools of ourselves.

The unmentionable answer was, of course, that Blackie had made a decision.

A cat will stand for a long time at an opened door and consider the immediate sensory arguments for and against going out: wind in the ears, rain, cold, snow on the ground, dogs, planes, sunshine, squirrels, and the condition of the litter box inside. The weights of these matters nudge the cat in one direction or the other, or, more often, in both directions until a human foot pushes him firmly out onto the steps. If the decision is negative, an experienced cat will go back to bed, sometimes for the whole month of February, while a young cat may ask to have the door reopened twenty times in the course of a single rainy day, to see if things have changed, but the decision process is the same. It's a decision we can allow a cat to make, simple and physical and based on observable factors: it is raining and in the past when I went out in the rain I got my feet wet; I don't like rain so I will stay in. This is no more complicated than deciding whether or not to scratch an ear—and I've seen cats undecided about that, too. If we're going to admit independent volition in animals, and Descartes begrudged them even that, insisting that all animal behavior was as automated as digestion, then we have to allow them to act on past experience and what they can see and hear at the moment.

But a cat does not make New Year's resolutions. A cat does not sit in the bushes one day and decide, without pressure of any kind, to stop being a vicious renegade with a price (we were going to give Terry a beer) on his head and turn himself into the mildest of house cats. Precious few humans are capable of this decision; our habitual criminals tend to stay criminal, and even our own simple resolutions, such as spending more time with the children, tend to fade by Groundhog Day. But leaving aside the effort of will involved in changing one's whole personality and behavior instantly and permanently, the intellectual leap is beyond him.

We know perfectly well that a cat doesn't have the kind of brain that could conceive of itself as a different creature from the one it is now, and take steps to become that creature. We are, surely, the only animal self-conscious enough to inspect our behavior and wonder if life would be more satisfying if we changed it: a cat can't imagine life as a different sort of cat any more than it can imagine life as a rhinoceros.

Even a very young human child can say to itself, "Maybe if I were a better boy my mother would be nicer to me and this would make me happier." No animal can say this. A dog can learn that if he sits when he's told to sit he'll get a pat on the head, but he can't suppose it before it's ever happened; dogs may want to please, but they aren't supposed to suppose.

Blackie cannot have thought things over and decided to become Basil.

What, then, did he think—or should I say "think"? What did happen? As swiftly as a werewolf changing back into human form with the blood of his midnight rampages still wet on his claws, he became a different cat, a cat of peace and sofa cushions, and in time even the other cats forgot his outlaw days and allowed him to curl among them in a patchwork heap, and no outsider, looking them over, could have guessed for which of these a man was coming with a gun.

2

Smart Like Us

When humans address the question of nonhuman intelligence, what we ask is, "How close is this creature's mind to ours?" Naturally it can come only so close and no closer, but our mind is the standard of perfection against which all imperfect, lesser minds must be measured. Then we make up tests to see just how far inferior cats are to humans at solving human puzzles; when the cats pose us feline puzzles we are not obliged to solve them, nor to call it failure if we fail to. Our tests measure the kind of persistence and cleverness valuable to humans in a modern, human world, because if not of use to us, then of what use at all?

We do not test for adaptability, or consider it a form of intelligence, because we're in charge here: humans don't need adaptability because humans call the shots, and adapting is the necessity of those below. We don't test for the capacity for contentment, because contentment is the enemy of progress; a contented human, if there were such a thing, would be useless to society, even a threat. We don't test for physical competence, because next to the warthog we're the most incompetent creature alive; therefore it simply doesn't count, an odd notion in a society that makes millionaires of its ballplayers.

Top criterion for true humanoid achievement is the use of

tools. We feel that using tools is pretty fancy stuff, possible only for smart people like us, and it never enters our minds that it might be smarter still if we were so sufficient in ourselves that we didn't need to use separate tools—if we were our own tools. In 1950 a four-month-old kitten climbed the Matterhorn with a group of mountaineers. It was the only member of the party without climbing and safety equipment. Is it, in the eye of eternity, really nobler to have invented the crampon than not to have needed the thing in the first place?

Besides tools, we admire as intelligence the concept of work. Being so ill-equipped for the world, we have to do a good deal of work just to survive, and since we do it, it must be a sign of intelligence, this submersion of natural inclination in order to accomplish a task. In animals, this usually boils down to working for us, at jobs we want done. Dogs understand work, and often seem to take the same self-important pleasure in it that we do, enjoying it as much for its own sake as for the praise attached. The bird dog brings us the bird, never thinking to eat it himself, and takes pride in the job well done. The elephant, considered an animal genius, seems to understand working for us and even to enjoy it, its little eyes twinkling merrily as it helps us destroy the forests that shelter its fellows. It even helps us trap wild elephants, herding them into stockades and then disciplining and instructing them in their future duties to man. Most people find this charming as well as intellectual.

The cat, a lesser being, does not work for us. It catches mice, but not for us, not as a job, though it may bring us one as a gift, freely offered and not because we asked. Task and obligation are not catly concepts. In the building of Grand Coulee Dam a cat was useful, taking a string tied to its tail along a winding drainpipe so that the engineers could pull a cable through it; what cat could resist exploring a winding drainpipe? No one supposes it wanted to be useful, or took any interest in dams; our separate interests, just for a moment, happened to cross.

They don't often. I have read, though I'm not sure I believe it, that in Vietnam the United States Army undertook to make cats on leashes lead foot soldiers through the night jungles, using their magical eyes to help us win our war. The project had to be abandoned because the cats kept playing with the pack straps of the soldiers in front, stopping to strop their claws on the soldiers' boots, and knocking off work altogether when it rained. It's rare that the cat's concept of fun coincides with the human concept of work; when the human tries to do paperwork, all the cat sees is a person wasting on a sheet of paper valuable attention that might better be spent on cats; when the human digs a row of holes in which to plant daffodils, the cat follows along using the holes for feline purposes and then filling them neatly in again.

We never ask—it would be sentimental to ask—what the purpose of intelligence is to its user, how successful the cat is to itself as a cat. We ask how successful it would be as a human. We ask it to prove that it could build a better mousetrap, perhaps forgetting that it doesn't need to; it is a better mousetrap. It never seems to occur to us that a cat, if it were human, might not want to learn to program in COBOL but instead to compose songs or dance with the Bolshoi or translate its dreams into numbers that win the lottery. We're disappointed in it when it doesn't bother to solve our puzzles, or push the right buttons to get out of a cage in which, contrary to instructions, it decided to take a nap.

One thing we used to know for certain about the lesser forms of life: they can't talk. Speech, human speech, we ardently believe, is the one utter necessity for abstract thought and the crowning glory that distinguishes the human mind from all other "minds." Lacking speech, an animal cannot entertain concepts. It's impossible, for instance, that both the Siamese Morgan and the new little black cat, being young and inexperienced, tried to play with the letter O. Both of them, on separate occasions, saw it, one of the big decorative capitals used to break up a page of print, and tried to roll it off the page. They ignored the F, the L, the

T, as being too angular, but they pawed for quite a while at the rollable O before they realized they'd been duped and gave up. Without the word *round*, they cannot entertain the thought "round," and this can't be allowed to have happened.

Without speech nothing can exist but the here and now, the concrete, the immediate sensory impression. Speech *is* thought. Without it, an animal's world is reduced to heat and cold, hunger and thirst, sex and reproduction: the rest is silence.

Consider Betsy, a most unremarkable cat. My daughter brought her home, a wretched scrap of alley flotsam with patches of white and patches of gray stripes, and she ate, washed up, and stayed. A nice enough cat and immaculate in her personal habits, but not the kind that impresses itself on a cat household; I more or less ignored her.

One evening I was scraping carrots into the sink and Betsy jumped up onto the counter. This was surprising; unlike all my cats she never jumped onto counters or the dinner table, having apparently made herself a set of rules for household behavior that never occurred to anyone else, least of all me. She stepped delicately into the sink, gazed greenly up at me to be sure she had my attention, and squatted and urinated.

"*Betsy!*" Betsy the prissy, Betsy of the perfect manners—in the *sink*? I raised my hand to smack her and she sprang onto the floor and raced toward the laundry room. I chased her. Glancing over her shoulder to see that I was still on her trail, she led me to the cat pan and stopped in front of it and looked up at me. She lifted a curled paw in disgust. It was a mess. I had been busy. I had neglected to change the litter.

I apologized, I cleaned the pan, I went back to the carrots. But I was shaken.

Consider the necessary train of thought, or "thoughts":

1. The woman changes the litter pan.
2. It needs changing badly, so she must have forgotten.

3. If I remind her, she'll change it.
4. How can I remind her? Just pacing back and forth meowing, or scratching the furniture, or nipping her ankle, will direct her attention to me but not to the litter pan.
5. How can I say, specifically, "litter pan" to her in a way she understands?
6. With a symbolic gesture. I will get her attention, and then demonstrate the problem to her.
7. Then she'll change it.

I don't know whether my chasing her was part of the plan, so she could lead me to the laundry room, or a spontaneous addition when she saw she had overestimated my intelligence and further explanation was necessary.

Those who have spent time in a country where they didn't speak the language know the difficulty of conveying a problem not in the same room, an invisible problem, even with hands to gesture with. Your car has broken down, but how to explain a car when there is no car in sight? Even given pencil and paper and hands to draw with, how to explain that the car won't run? It takes very little genuine intelligence to say "My car broke down" to someone who understands the words; inventing a symbolic demonstration is high-order effort.

When a cat wants a door opened, it pantomimes opening the door, reaches for the doorknob or hooks a paw under the edge and glares around at the people. But the door is there, and means door, directly, as refrigerator means food, while urinating in the sink only symbolizes a dirty litter pan, the way setting fire to a piece of striped cotton means "Americans go home." We like to think we hold a monopoly on this symbolic reference to the intangible; in fact, we insist on it.

Roger Brown, in *Words and Things*, says, "Most people are determined to hold the line against animals. Grant them the ability to make linguistic reference and they will be putting in a claim for minds and souls. The whole phyletic scale will come trouping into Heaven demanding immortality for every tadpole and hippopotamus. Better be firm now and make it clear that man alone can *use language and make reference*. There is a qualitative difference of mentality separating us from animals."

The italics are mine. Betsy couldn't use our spoken words, lacking the vocal setup, but she used what physical equipment she did have. And if she wasn't "referring" to the litter pan—if I were a scientist it would be worth my diploma to suppose she was—then we have to assume that this cat of almost irritatingly hygienic habit once in her life suffered from an aberrant impulse, a kind of psychobiologic twitch, that made her risk a beating by jumping into the sink and committing an unheard-of indecency right under my hands. When screamed at she coincidentally ran toward the litter pan; the fact that it needed cleaning is inadmissible evidence, since I couldn't retest her to prove that she *wouldn't* run toward a pan that *didn't* need cleaning; science is hard work.

Always ascribe intelligent behavior to coincidence, however bizarre. Anecdote is not evidence, and no valid results can be taken from a test set up by the animal itself and not by us; only human testing is conclusive.

In the animal laboratory of the Department of Psychology at Columbia University, Audrey M. Shuey worked with eighty-two kittens for nearly a year and a half, during which time they grew into eighty-two deeply confused cats.

She constructed a cage within a cage. The inner cage had the food in it, and a door; the outer cage had three electrical pressure plates in the floor, programmable by the operator to open the door to the food when properly stepped on.

In the beginning the door opened whenever any one plate was stepped on, then if any two plates, then any three. Each kitten was given five minutes to pass the test, and to Shuey's apparent surprise they didn't all buckle down to work immediately, but frittered away the precious minutes "sitting or washing, playing with tail, pawing at shadow, jumping, rolling over, rubbing against the walls." Sometimes they simply curled up and went to sleep, indicating a lack of ambition repulsive to the human mind.

It took them anywhere from nine to 136 sessions to learn to step on one plate to get dinner. To step on two plates took from one to seventy tries, and to step on all three from one to 121. The kittens that came out best were "facing the inner door as they touched the plate accidentally and probably saw the door slide back." Shuey doesn't seem surprised by this, but it bears thinking about.

A cat knows nothing of electrical impulses that open doors from a distance, any more than Betsy, when she was shot by a neighbor a year after the sink incident, could have understood murder from thirty feet away. The fact that the kittens made the connection "step here and that door opens over there," though it was irrelevant to Shuey's question, seems rather clever. If I rub my ear and a fire truck passes by outside, I don't assume I've produced the fire truck by rubbing, but only because I've been told of the habits of fire trucks. Some of the kittens made an assumption and happened to be right.

They could have been wrong. A French writer reports on a cat and her kittens who always ate lunch with the family, on the table. One day, just as the platter of pork chops was set on the table, there was a loud explosion in the gas pipes, frightening everyone. No damage was done, and the people resumed their lunch, but the cats stayed in hiding. Some weeks later, with peace long re-established, pork chops were served again, and when the platter was set on the table the cats panicked and scattered. Pork chops do not cause explosions, but given that the cats' ignorance of gas pipes is greater even than mine, the assumption was sound enough.

Understanding cause and effect isn't really the high-level thinking we've made of it, and doesn't depend on knowing exactly how the effect is caused; if I answer a ringing telephone, I expect a voice at the other end, though I couldn't explain how it gets there. When Blueberry and I lived in a third-floor walkup, the snarl of a buzzer meant that someone was coming to visit: I pressed the button that released the catch on the downstairs door, and after a suitable interval company came in, gasping from the climb. I didn't tell the cat that a fellow tenant had lost her key, and I had promised to let her in when she rang. She did, and I did, and thought no more about it. Blueberry sat by the door and waited. Nobody came. She paced. She glowered at me. She hooked her paw under the door and rattled it angrily. Buzzer means company; where the hell is company?

Cats have less trouble than we like to think with this much thinking.

Meanwhile, back at Columbia, Shuey pressed on. In the next phase of the exam, the cats had to step on all three plates and then go back and step on one of the first two a second time. Then on all three once and the first two twice, then on all three twice but without repeating the immediately previous plate. Shuey then added a fourth plate, so that getting the food required the proper stepping-on of plates twelve times. Then she arranged to have the door open only if the plates were stepped on in a preprogrammed order.

The natural way for a cat to get its dinner is to lie in wait, to stalk, and to pounce; putting up with this electronic dance seems uncommonly good-natured of them if not necessarily intelligent.

Four of the cats did brilliantly and one poor dodo took 271 tries to get through the first basic series. (Perhaps the food in the inner cage was something he hated. One of my cats hates kidneys, another won't touch liver.) The study, when Shuey finally ran out of plates and quit, proved conclusively that some cats are more intelligent than others. Or hungrier. Or less interested in alternative activities like chasing their tails.

Since she noted that eighty percent of the cats stepped on the plates with their front paws first, it also proved that more cats walk forward than backward.

It's interesting to consider that Shuey's intelligence, or even sanity, was not under question at any time, nor was she asked, as a control, to pass a test of the cats' devising. Crossing the room without stepping on the floor, for instance.

In recent years studies of animal intelligence have shifted from the ability to manipulate traps to the ability to use language. Not to communicate, which is primitive, but to use *real* language. *Our* language. Words. Cats are off the hook, primates are on, and gorillas and chimpanzees are crowding our solitary superiority by talking to us in the human sign language. Where now is our "qualitative difference of mentality separating us from the animals"? Not only do they learn to make the signs, which really would seem a simple enough intellectual feat, and the hand sign "hunger" not too far above a cat scratching at the refrigerator door, but they also learn to put the words together into groups that, when we use them ourselves, we call "thoughts." They ask for comforting hugs when things go wrong, and asking for them in a language *we've* invented seems very much classier indeed than, for instance, a cat asking for a comforting lap in the language natural to a cat.

These primates say insulting things about each other. And they tell lies.

Lucy, the famous signing chimp, was asked by her trainer if she was responsible for that pile of feces (for all their brilliance, they're as hard to housebreak as a human) in the middle of the floor. She said no. She said the trainer had done it himself.

A lie is a sophisticated concept. First to learn the words, then to arrange them in groups, and then to use them to say something contrary to fact in order to blame another for one's own crime—now, *that's* human. That's getting uncomfortably close to home. Carry this thing much further and it could raise all sorts of questions few of us are pure enough to face.

Luckily we're dealing only with primates here, since nothing else has fingers, and if we have to move over and make room in the intellectual community we won't have to make very much room.

It may really be that primates are smarter than other animals because they're the most like us; certainly we like to think so, having had to swallow the theory of a common ancestor. And certainly they are like us. Meeting, through smudged glass, the eyes of a gorilla in the zoo, we feel the quivering shock of recognition that runs through every fiber: an animal not ours but *us*. The endless fascination of a cat's eyes lies in the difference. A cat is not us. The cat is inside there, and its mind is working, but how?

We've never even considered inventing a practical speech for animals with neither hands nor voice boxes, and if we did, how would we teach it to a cat, or answer, since we lack a cat's movable equipment as much as it lacks ours? Our deficiency in the matter clinches the cat's inferior mentality.

Speechlessness doesn't stop the cat from telling lies. Derek Tangye's cat Monty lied. In *Somewhere a Cat is Waiting*, he tells us that he and his wife were packing to go on a trip when Monty came to them with a painful limp, hobbling on three legs, unable to touch paw to floor. They called the vet, the vet came and examined the cat and said there was nothing at all wrong with him, and Monty stalked huffily away on all four feet.

A horse, no intellectual giant, who has gone lame and been let off work because of it, may fake going lame again, but this is only cause and effect at its simplest. Suitcases are only cause and effect: all cats know that their appearance means the people are going away, and some cats sulk, or hide, or hunker down inside the suitcase to make it impossible to pack. But apparently Monty, to whom it had never happened, supposed, like Boston Blackie supposing a reformed life, that if he were ill the people would cancel their trip. And apparently he also knew when his bluff had been called. And certainly he told a deliberate lie.

The naturalist W. H. Hudson said, "Cats are mentally near to us; their brains function even as ours do." Somewhere in there beyond the language barrier.

Lately it has occurred to our researchers that, if we can't

teach cats a real language, at least we can write down their own unschooled and primitive utterances and assign them meanings. On a recent Public Broadcast special I admired a massive computer console digesting a program that analyzed the sounds of cats; each sound was recorded and broken down and assigned a meaning, and when the project is complete we will have a written language for the cat. It's simple enough, according to this research, since the cat has only fifteen different sounds to be combined into twenty-five different vocalizations. "Meow" is actually two words, "me," a greeting, and "ow," meaning "keep your distance," used more with people than with other cats.

Unfortunately, in a recent book, *How to Talk to Your Animals*, Jean Craighead George says that "meow" with the accent on the "ow" means "follow me," while the same word drawn out and unaccented is a whine of protest.

And of course in order to carry out this translation we'll have to search out cats that say "meow" at all, though I did meet one once. It was unnerving, like having a rooster walk up and say "cock-a-doodle-doo." And having compiled a glossary of terms for cats that use the sounds that English-speakers think of as cat sounds, we can turn our attention to other countries, since the Chinese think their cats say "ming" and what we hear as "purr" the French hear as "ron-ron." In the end the cats will be no better than the humans, separated from cats in other lands by separate languages.

My own unscientific feeling is that the language of the cat is as individual as fingerprints, and the wonder of it is that it's understood by us and by other cats without anything resembling a commonly agreed-on vocabulary. And, being more music than word, it cannot be transliterated. We can represent the opening of a symphony with "da-da-da *dah*," but that isn't at all what it sounds like, and the only reason we recognize the syllables is that we've heard the thing the way it belongs, as music. We cannot decipher what Beethoven "meant" and proceed from there to assume that other composers would mean the same thing from the same notes.

Some cats use their voices rarely and some never stop yammering except in sleep; are we to suppose that the silent ones aren't communicating and the noisy ones are? Not necessarily. I have here a young Siamese female who, since she was neutered, says almost nothing. When she speaks, it's a syllable somewhere between "mah" and "wan," and it means "want." She has a high opinion of my intelligence, and never goes to the cupboard for food or the door for out; she comes to me and says "want," and I'm supposed to understand. The Persian Barney speaks even less frequently, his single "meh" being forced up from his very toes with obvious difficulty, and depending on location it means either that breakfast is late or he wants the tap in the basin turned on.

Neither cat is unintelligent or uncommunicative.

The new little black cat never opens her mouth to say anything, but speaks in her throat, to herself, trotting up and down stairs and in and out of closets chirping and murmuring and exclaiming in a kind of watered-silk pattern of sound that can make the possessor of mere English feel as mute and flightless as a turnip. This is interior monologue, though, intended to communicate with no one but herself; for speech she has a long, wavery, pointed tail of such expressive grace that it must be a perfect poem for those with the sense to understand its voice.

Then there's Corvo, a stout elderly Siamese, who speaks in deep chest tones, as if from a bellows, in an infinite variety of yet-to-be-invented vowels, comparable maybe to an unmilked cow or a French horn with a sore throat. It sounds consistently gloomy, and is capable of roaring amplification, but it's used mostly as a greeting, or to suggest the making of a lap, or to inquire after missing members of the family.

Sidney, probably the least intelligent, has the largest vocabulary. He believes that a cat can penetrate a windowpane with a bird on the other side of it by standing on his hind legs and swimming violently on the glass with his front paws, and he has believed this for seventeen years in the face of overwhelming evidence to the contrary, but he has a marvelous range of vocal expression. Some of it means something. A booming spectral moan means he doesn't like riding in cars, and a cantankerous "a-yow" means he's about to use the litter pan. A sharp nasal "yan" means it's twenty after three in the morning and time to get up; this is followed by ducklike food cries of "skwap skwap" as he hustles down the stairs urging us to follow and serve breakfast. (The fact that he keeps on hoping, though he never has been fed at that hour and often gets things thrown at him, speaks poorly for his learning ability, and if he'd had to step twelve times on electric pressure plates to get his food he would have starved.) However, most of what Sidney says is apparently meaningless, a kind of feline skat or do-wap with dozens of different grunts, squeaks, cries, and murmurs that seem to be just Sidney talking to hear the sound of his own voice, as a human might sing in the shower. Sometimes he goes down in the basement and sings to enjoy the hollow concrete acoustics.

There is no cat "language." Painful as it is for us to admit, they don't need one.

We depend quite woefully on speech to understand each other even slightly. When the leaders of great nations get together to sort out the problems of the world, they have no way of knowing what's in each other's minds without an interpreter, and if the interpreter has to duck out to go to the bathroom, the great leaders are left sitting there twiddling their key chains and avoiding each other's eyes until he comes back. We've been talking to each other for so long that our more efficient lines of communication have withered away. Granted, cats can't discuss the future deployment of missiles, but consider the advantages of not needing to discuss them.

A cat can tell us infinitely more than we can tell a cat, and certainly more than the great leaders can tell each other across the language barrier. A cat has, for instance, thirty different muscles in its ears, making them expressive of the subtlest shades of interest and disapproval, while we have only six and most of us can't use any of them. If we live with a cat, and the cat holds its ears in a certain position, we know without thinking about it that the cat is cross, or that it hears something across the room. How do we know? We just do. Perhaps we aren't so dense after all.

The whole cat is an instrument of communication. It has forty more bones in its flexible body than we do; the bones of its spine are connected by muscle instead of ligament, so that even its back communicates. Its movable whiskers inform us, and the pupils of its eyes expand and contract with mood as well as with light. The hairs of its back and tail rise up for threat or fear, accompanied by the international Esperanto of growls and hisses. A sound that Colette spells "Mouek mouek mouek, Ma-a-a-a" and B. Kliban spells "wacka wacka wacka" means "I see a bird, and I wish I could catch it, but birds are hard to catch, not worth making a fool of myself over, and that makes me furious."

Without trying to decipher the meaning of "meow" we can understand a good deal of cat. How does the cat understand us? No mere human can begin to realize the scope of smell for animals that can use it; it's a whole lost language for us. Through a haze of cigarette smoke, garlic, bath soap, and cologne the cat can smell on our skin subtle pH changes from fear or anger and heaven knows what else. Any illness changes our scent, grief changes it, and the cat reacts, sometimes with motherly comforting and sometimes with panic and anger. Posture, energy level, tone of voice; all this is easily read. And language? Words?

Does not being able to speak them mean not being able to understand? Conservative science holds that human speech in the cats' ears is only a formless river of intonation and inflection, and no cat can make the intellectual connection between the sound itself and the indicated object, only learn from long experience, from the speaker's body language and tone, to make a few tentative inferences: "Bad!" doesn't mean "bad" but is only a sound, like a growl, that comes from the human when you rip up the couch. "Here, kitty, kitty, kitty" is a sound preliminary to dinner. The dog that comes when called doesn't understand his name as meaning *him*, only as a sound that means his owner wants him, accompanied by subtle tonal qualities that help him identify it; he may not even recognize it in another's voice. A name is a word. Animals can't grasp the concept "word."

Gone with the Wind was playing on television. Barney was sound asleep. The little girl was riding around on her pony, about to break her neck, and for several minutes the set rang with cries of "Bonnie! Bonnie!" The cat woke up and looked at the television, but nothing on the set related to him. "Bonnie!" they cried, and he turned and looked at me, first inquiringly, then angrily. Someone, somewhere, was teasing him. "Bonnie!" He got down off the couch and left the room in a huff, and I remembered his first owner and her soft southern voice. "Bahney," she called him. "Baahney." If I hadn't had the spellings in my mind, I couldn't have told the sounds apart. And in Barney's ears it was a word, and meant whatever he thinks of as "him," and had nothing to do with recognized inflection or tone; he has never even met Clark Gable.

If "Barney," then what else? I'm not suggesting we can explain physics or calculus or the Roman Empire to a cat, because there's no way to make a cat care enough to want to learn about them, a problem shared with many humans. But what indeed are the limits? If we say often enough to a cat, "Do you want to go *out*?" and then open the door, many cats I have known learn to go to the door and say, even if it's a sound they never use elsewhere, "Ow." Are they saying "out," or is this pure coincidence?

If the cat wanted to learn, how much could we teach it? But why should it want to learn? A cat is different, a cat is not us, a cat is satisfied to be a cat and speak as a cat.

I've known only one cat that seemed to long for human speech, and in this I'm being outrageously sentimental and subjective. His name is Flanagan and he's one of my sis-

ter's horde, a beautiful cat with the softest blue-gray fur and
round yellow eyes with an intense, yearning expression. A
cat of passionate moods, when he feels loving it's not
enough to watch a human from across the room and
squeeze his eyes shut; laps are not enough. He scrambles
straight up toward the face, clawing his way up trousers
and shirt and throwing his forelegs around the neck in a
desperate hug, his body pressed against the chest, and purrs
raggedly and nips and licks the face in a fit of thwarted
passion quite awkward for a human to accept from a cat.
Even in his less emotional moments there's something ur-
gent and frustrated about Flannie in his human contacts,
and even the most pragmatic among us struggles with
thoughts of reincarnation and princes enchanted into toads.

Not that he doesn't enjoy other cats. He used to come
down to my house every day to sing with Sidney. These
sessions were enormously satisfying to both cats; he and
Sid faced each other off on the porch and yowled and yo-
deled after the manner of the pregame show of rival tomcats. Both were neutered, and unthreatened, and secure in
their territories; it was a combination of concert and the war
games of little boys. Flanagan had a fine talent for swelling
up, not just the fur but the entire cat, like a blowfish, to astonishing size and weaving his head gruesomely while he
yowled. No blows were ever offered. After twenty minutes
or so, Sidney would come back inside and Flan would go
on home.

Unhappily, after several months Sidney got bored. He
stopped going outside when Flanagan gave his invitational
calls. He is old, and would rather sleep than sing.

Then Flanagan would hook his paws into the screen door
and stare beseechingly in at me, trying to leap out through
his own eyes and tell me how badly he wanted Sidney to
come out. I would drag Sid from his chair and throw him
out the door; Flanagan would moan hopefully, and Sid
would turn his back in silence and ask to come inside
again. It was very sad.

Then I had to move away from the little house. The furniture left in a truck, the cats and pictures in the car, and the next day I went back with a broom and a bucket for the final cleanup.

Flanagan heard my car and came hurrying down the driveway and across the porch and hooked his paws into the screen door. I let him in. "He's not here," I said. "He's gone." Flanagan scattered in panic through the empty house and ran around every room and closet, over and over. Nothing. He came back to me and stared up, searching my face.

He wasn't looking in my face for Sidney; he was looking for an explanation. He was straining to split open his limitations and ask "Where is he?" and understand the answer. Yet how can a cat, who has never heard an explanation, want one so badly?

I could only shake my head and gesture vaguely at the empty room.

There was always something embarrassing in my dealings with Flanagan. Once or twice it flicked across my mind to offer him a pencil and paper: if he couldn't say it, maybe he could write it down. It was hard to fend off the sense that inside that gray fur a frantic human was waving his arms and pointing to the adhesive tape across his mouth.

Able to limp only the smallest distance into the minds of the speechless, we comfort ourselves with the thought that there can't be much to find in any case. A twitching collection of nerves and reflexes. A dark hole illuminated only by flickering reactions to stimuli like heat and food.

With the signing primates we feel we've made some progress into the darkness, and admire the apes being slow and clumsy as humans over cats being competent as cats. Probably there's a distinction, though it's hard for the unscientific to see, between teaching them sign language and dressing them in funny hats to photograph them eating birthday cake. Probably we've learned something. Probably they're almost smart like us.

A cat sits on our rug with its tail wrapped around its feet and its eyes focused on a point in the middle air, and we tell ourselves that its mind is an emptiness unimaginable to the clever human, who, we like to believe, spends its idle hours musing on political economy, existentialism, and the lesser comedies of Aristophanes. Take away our words and we wouldn't be able to think of anything at all, so it stands to reason that a cat, having no words, thinks of nothing.

Our real need of speech is just to tell each other about the far-off times and spaces that distract us so: over there, back then, last week, next year, Washington, Syria. But to a cat space is easy, space is only territory, contained and known; and time is easy, time is where the cat is sitting now. Spring speaks to its loins, breakfast time speaks to its stomach, but time past is a flicker of dateless memories without perspective and future time doesn't matter at all. At the point where time and space meet the cat sits on the rug, cupped in the immediate moment like a single note struck on the piano, and what we call intelligence is of less importance to its life than the dust motes in a shaft of sun.

T. S. Eliot says the musing cat is contemplating his secret name, the name that contains the compact essence of the individual cat, the kernel of his unknowable self. Mr. Eliot was being whimsical, but he was right just the same.

3

People With Cats

Very few people have no opinions about cats. Even those who have never known a cat personally, scarcely even spoken to one, feel strongly and sometimes hysterically on the subject. Consider Buffon, the great eighteenth-century naturalist, and his cool scientific detachment: "Many people . . . raise cats solely for their own amusement, which I find utterly abnormal . . . a malicious streak in [cats], and a naturally perverse dishonest character . . . ruthless . . . fawning and opportunistic . . . the same devious techniques as any human thief . . . shifty eyes . . . seek human company exclusively for their own benefit . . . mothers occasionally become unnaturally cruel and eat their own dear offspring alive . . . systematically malicious . . ."

It's rather a compliment, really; we can hardly imagine him working up such a lather about, for instance, sheep.

Equally detached, the zoologist Scheitlin rhapsodizes, "The forehead has a truly poetic curve; indeed, the whole of the skeleton is beautiful and suggests a highly mobile animal, particularly well suited for all graceful and undulating movements." We have all known cats so graceless they could barely undulate across the floor without tripping over it, but there's no arguing with a man who finds even their bones enchanting.

People who hate cats tend to be proud of the fact, and brag about it as if it proved something honest and straightforward in their natures. Nobody brags about hating dogs. To hate dogs would be mean-spirited and peculiarly unpatriotic; dogs are a very American concept, fraternal, hearty, and unpretentious, while cats are inscrutable like the wily Oriental and elitist like the European esthete. In advertising, cats turn up selling perfume (wily) and expensive rugs and furniture (elitist), while dogs sell such solid family values as station wagons, life insurance, and sporting goods.

Men who hate both cats and women say cats are like women, and refer to even the most swaggeringly potent tomcat as "she."

Cats are held to be sneaky. They earn their livings sneaking. Dogs in the wild catch their prey like good old boys, outnumbering it and running it down in broad daylight, and they can make as much noise as they please in the process. Cats in the wild don't hunt in packs, though lions may cooperate, and they can't outrun their prey; they're fast, but only in the short sprint. They have to surprise their dinner by creeping quietly, waiting patiently, and springing accurately. Sometimes they hunt by night, too, which is manifestly unfair. None of this is very attractive to the human mind. The human mind may even remember Smilodon with his six-inch saber teeth, who could probably sneak as softly as any house cat in spite of being fourteen feet long, and his dinner might have been a friend of ours. When he isn't hunting, the domestic cat is anything but sneaky, and a pair of them in a hurry down a flight of uncarpeted stairs makes as much noise as a pair of adolescent male humans on the same journey. Hunting, he has to sneak; you don't catch mice by stamping your feet and shouting about your intentions. And since they say we took him on in the first place to catch mice, it seems ungrateful to complain about his *modus operandi*.

It's commonly said that cats are never attached to their people and hang around only because they're fed. The phrase "cupboard love" was coined for cats. This is odd since cats are notoriously finicky eaters, easily put off their feed by emotional upsets, and often better able than dogs to supplement their diet with a catch. And every cat household has known a cat that blatantly preferred a member of the family who never fed him to the one who did. Pet dogs, presumably, get fed, and goldfish, and gerbils, and no one accuses them of cupboard love. It goes with the legend of the independent cat; if not for food, why would nature's freest spirit stay at home?

Konrad Lorenz, pioneer animal-watcher, says in *King Solomon's Ring*, "All other domestic animals, like some slaves of ancient times, became house servants only after having served a term of true imprisonment, all, that is, with the exception of the cat, for the cat is not really a domesticated animal and his chief charm lies in the fact that, even today, he still walks by himself. Neither the dog nor the cat is a slave, but only the dog is a friend—granted, a submissive and servile 'friend' . . ."

It's a strange notion he has of friendship, with one party doing all the commanding and the other all the obeying, and we might wonder how he'd feel about his dog if it started ordering him to sit and heel and fetch. It's a strange notion of slavery too, which remains nonetheless slavery even when the slave enjoys it thoroughly.

"The cat still walks by itself." Ah, yes, we do cherish the thought. The undomesticated cat, free as the wind, beholden to no one, waving his wet wild tail as he moves on down the lonesome road. The more our own lives are fenced around with obligations and family ties and jobs to show up for, the more we dwell on the dream of the unfettered cat. Cat-haters hate him for it, cat-lovers love him for it. Like the jolly miller on the River Dee, he cares for nobody, no, not he, and nobody cares for him. When things get sticky he can simply leave town like the beloved imaginary cowboy of the Old West, riding away toward the blue hills and leaving only a puff of dust as a forwarding address.

We could pick genuine wild animals to envy, eagles and wolves and mountain goats, but they live remote from our houses, and besides, we sensibly see their lives as pretty arduous. Not free like cat and cowboy but beset by blizzards and hunters and young to rear. We see the cat as needing nothing, in spite of the fact that the actual independent cats we run across are wretchedly thin and miserable, with an estimated maximum life expectancy of two years. That has nothing to do with it; the *spirit* of the cat, like an invisible flame hovering over its starving body, is independent and rides away into the sunset the way we would ride if we could, singing nonchalantly of the girl we left behind.

It's curious that throughout our history together, with no apparent effort, people have been able to think of the cat simultaneously as the guardian spirit of the hearth and home, and as the emblem of freedom, independence, and rootlessness.

Capriciously, we keep them at home as guardian spirits or abandon them as independent. People otherwise decent and kindly throw away countless thousands of cats and kittens to die slowly of hideous hardships; cats, after all, can take care of themselves, cats are not domestic animals at all.

The cat is neither cowboy nor spirit, but flesh and blood, a small predator adrift in a world of garbage cans and highways, domestic now for thousands of years. Unknowable, maybe, but ours. Under modern conditions it survives on its own only briefly, with pain and difficulty. The fact that it treats us as equals rather than gods doesn't mean it can find its way in our world without help.

We owe them help. In spite of all they've suffered at our hands they seem to like us, of their own free will, a compliment our rapacious bullying species can't afford to ignore. What other animal sits with us because it chose to?

Wild dogs live in groups and give their leader, until the time comes to challenge his leadership, an unquestioning military loyalty; domestic dogs offer the same religious devotion to the human they consider their leader. According to Lorenz, dogs of primarily coyote extraction spread this feeling out over most of the humans that cross their paths, while dogs with more wolf in them concentrate on one. Either way, it's natural for humans to applaud this taste in idols.

I've been lucky in being loved by some cats, but I've never had one who seemed to think that, aside from my presumed ability to improve the weather if only I would, I was any bigger, stronger, or smarter than I am. Cat people find it soothing to be loved in spite of their faults; dog people find it even more soothing to be considered faultless.

Because of their instinctive reaction to leadership, dogs are forced to like us, whoever we may be; they have no choice. The cat can choose and, having been chosen, we have a right to be pleased.

Many of us aren't. Something in the cat's attitude, or in its eyes, disturbs us, and we invent all sorts of plausible-sounding excuses to explain our uneasiness.

One prime reason cat-haters give for hating cats is that they kill birds. Even people who can't tell a nuthatch from a raven complain about it. To listen to them, a cat barely needs to stroll outdoors for birds to keel over in midair for miles around. Catching a bird isn't easy, as anyone knows who has ever chased a loose canary around the living room, and if the canary has the whole outside world to fly around in it's simply impossible. Let the bird-lover just try it himself and see. Cats may cull the elderly and the genetically incapable, the way wolves weed out the caribou, but this makes life easier for the healthy remainder, since shrinking habitat is much the fiercest pressure on bird populations.

Wildlife managers estimate that birds kill more birds than cats do. I believe it, having watched a blue jay murder a nest full of baby wrens outside my window. The wrens had successfully routed the cats from their whole end of the yard, but they were helpless against the jay. They darted back and forth shrieking; I ran out yelling and waving my arms. The jay, for no reason but wantonness, pounded the babies to bloody shreds and flew away cawing. I never saw the parent wrens again, and the cats were once more free to walk across that part of the lawn.

Birds know more about cats than bird-lovers do. The sedentary robin, checking the grass for worms, flies only eight or ten feet when he sees the cat approaching and then goes on with his search, removing himself from time to time until the cat gets bored and leaves.

I hung the bird feeder over the back steps, just over the cats' heads. The old cats enjoyed watching and made no move, but young Morgan wanted one badly. She could hardly stand it, the fluttering toys, just barely out of reach; it was maddening. Once in a while she made a fool of herself leaping into the air and trying to catch one by clapping her paws together. Then they all flew into the maple tree and waited for five minutes while she chattered with frustration. But when a hawk made a pass at the feeder they vanished instantly and completely and the feeder stayed birdless for days, as if his passage had left a stain of terror across the air: it takes wings to catch wings.

We had a cat who got adopted by a bird. George the Second had once been chased and bitten by one of my sister's white mice, and this may have shaken his confidence or confused his sense of his role in life, and he was one of the peaceable grays to begin with. When the baby blue jay started eating out of his bowl on the porch George just backed away into a corner, looking baffled, and waited till it was finished. It was a very young bird, probably fallen from its nest and abandoned, and certainly it was a very resourceful one. It stayed on the porch, waiting for George's twice-daily bowl of cat food, and it ate first, and George twitched his tail and looked put-upon. It grew. It took to following George everywhere, on foot. Birds apparently learn their identities from their parents, and identify their parents as parents because they supply the food. George supplied the food, therefore he became father to a blue jay child, which presumably thought it was a cat.

What George thought was obvious. He was embarrassed, horribly embarrassed, to walk across the lawn with a yeeping, gaping baby bird trudging after him clamoring to be fed. He tried to be invisible, bending his knees and huddling his head down into his shoulders, and he lashed his tail with impotent disgust. In theory he could have turned around and atomized the cheeky little thing, but it wasn't acting very much like prey, and besides the white mouse had bitten him quite hard.

In time the jay grew up and went off to find its own food, but we always wondered what kind of life it had later, and whether it continued to think of itself as a cat, and how this would affect its chances for a sane and normal married life. George was enormously relieved when it left.

Every so often a state's bird-lovers will band together and try to get legislation enacted that will keep cats under control, duly licensed, and on their own property. In vetoing such a bill in Illinois, then-Governor Adlai Stevenson wrote, "It is the nature of cats to do a certain amount of unescorted roaming . . . Moreover, cats perform useful service, particularly in rural areas, in combating rodents— work they necessarily perform alone and without regard to property lines. The problem of cat versus bird is as old as time. If we attempt to resolve it by legislation, who knows but that we may be called upon to take sides as well in the age-old problems of dog versus cat, bird versus bird, or even bird versus worm."

Cats give legislators a lot to worry about. It's illegal in Natchez for a cat to drink beer, and illegal in Morrisburg, Louisiana, for a cat to chase a duck down the city streets.

Another common complaint is the cruelty of cats. They not only kill mice, they torture them first, apparently for the sheer pleasure of seeing them suffer.

Actually, the business of playing with the catch has to do with the education of kittens in mouse work, and however it may look from a distance, the cat isn't mangling the mouse, except psychologically; if it were a robin's egg it wouldn't break. Killing, when the time comes, is swift and immediate, with a quick bite to the base of the neck that severs the spinal cord, and until then the game has the secondary effect of giving the mouse a sporting chance. I've seen quite a lot of them escape from the dallying cat to the safety of their holes. When, in our relentless pursuit of hamburgers, we herd the gentle steer in terror to the abattoir to knock it on the head, it doesn't have the shadow of a chance, any more than the bull in the bullring after we've finished our game.

Not all cats play with their mice. Corvo the battling Siamese is the most efficient mouser I've ever watched. He springs from incredible distances, lands with pinpoint accuracy, and kills on landing. Then he hunkers down to eat. Corvo comes from a cattery, and his businesslike approach finishes off the widely held theory that a cat whose mother never showed it how may chase mice but can't kill them: no mice volunteered as demonstration models in the cattery.

The Siamese Morgan, on the other hand, *only* plays with mice. She's fond of things that move when she pats them, and keeps a supply of pecans under my desk for the purpose. Vacuuming, I gathered them up and put them in a bowl on the desk, and then forgot to put them back. Morgan found them, and had to scoop them all out one by one and knock them to the floor and roll them, muttering crossly to herself, back where they belong. She's a cat with a strong sense of order and the rightness of things, and would have made an excellent secretary.

She seems to think of mice as an outdoor pecan supply. She'll chivvy one out into an open space like the gravel driveway and pat it till it runs a few feet and then freezes. She follows it and with velvet paw pats it to make it move again. After a few minutes she begins to lose interest, her mind wanders and she looks away, and the mouse runs like hell. She looks back at the spot where it was, but it is gone, so she yawns and goes off to see if I've left the car windows open so she can take a nap.

Granted the mouse's nerves are probably shattered, but we can't worry about everything.

Still, the charge of deliberate cruelty is a heavy one, if we can believe the cat understands the mouse's sufferings, and we've all been comforted by cats who understand ours. But we are people, the cats' people, and a mouse in the cats' eyes is only a mouse. In *Hen's Teeth and Horses' Toes* Stephen Jay Gould quotes from St. George Mivart's *Genesis of Species*; Mivart holds that animals feel little if any pain, because physical suffering "depends greatly upon the mental condition of the sufferer. Only during consciousness does it exist, and only in the most highly organized men does it reach its acme. The author has been assured that the lower races of men appear less keenly sensitive to physical suffering than do more cultivated and refined human beings."

The British scientist feels himself as far superior, in his delicately nurtured nervous system, to the uneducated races as the cat does to the mouse. If primitive humans feel no pain, how much credit shall a cat give a mere mouse for sensitivity? The only charge we can pin on the cat is that it has advanced in empathy no further than a nineteenth-century scientist.

The defense rests.

And in any case it's pointless to argue; cat-hating is visceral.

We have a cat around the house in a different sense from having, or owning, a dog. Even the law recognizes this, and considers the dog as property, and subject to property laws of damage and recovery, but no rights attach to cat ownership. Domestic, yes; property, no.

The cat doesn't bolster our self-esteem, and we can't pretend it works for us; it is *around*, in the nonspecific way all animals used to be around. We've grown so wildly successful as a race that we've managed to set a wide space between ourselves and the rest of the creatures. Pouring cream into our breakfast coffee, we are far, far from the cow, and except for occasional parasites like the pigeon most of the creatures most of us see in our normal rounds are human. A dog, since it's come to live with us, is hardly an animal at all, but a cat flits across the back of the couch and, in defiance of orders, leaps to the top of the bookcase and flips her tail at us, an animal nearby but not totally under our control. Hardly under our control at all except as she pleases, the way once the plains and forests all around us were full of animals nearby and uncontrolled. Many people dislike being reminded of the past and our humble, sometimes precarious, place in it, but it may be good for us.

Cat-keeping nowadays is almost always pure self-indulgence; very few cats are essentially employed. Only a little while ago cats were working wherever we went, as they still are in Europe; the butcher had to have one, and the fishmonger, and all proper groceries had two, one for the shop and one for the cellar. But America, being fond of science, progress, and hygiene, passed laws saying cats were unscientific and unhygienic and can no longer live in or even stroll through places where food is kept or sold. The plump and cozy grocer's cat has been replaced by the sickening stench of rat poison and, occasionally, of poisoned rat rotting its heart out in some inaccessible corner. The farmer with his barnful of cats has been replaced by food production on a scale so dizzyingly vast and automated it's hard to imagine where the humble cat could fit in; perhaps they have giant robot cats.

Now the only working cats we see are in bookstores and antiques shops, where they sprawl in the display windows to strike the proper note of cultivated leisure.

It has been said that to respect the cat is the beginning of the esthetic sense, and at a stage of culture where utility governs all, mankind prefers the dog. We have time here for esthetics now; we can stop sleeping with our boots on and use our cats for subtle, impractical purposes.

We keep cats now for their otherness. A dog, a well-trained dog, can feel almost like an extension of ourselves, responsive and familiar as our own hands. A cat is not us; a cat is the Other. It's a mark of a mature civilization to be able to accept an other, and respect its differences without feeling threatened; it would do wonders for world affairs.

Some people are more temperamentally suited to cat-keeping than other people. In general, those whose souls rejoice in the power struggle and the conquest of nations get along badly with cats. Genghis Khan hated them, and Alexander the Great, and Julius Caesar, and Hitler is said to have thrown fits at the very word. Shortly after the battle of Wagram, Napoleon was on his way to bed when an aide-de-camp heard him screaming for help, and rushed to his bedroom to find the victorious commander half undressed and slashing his sword wildly at the wall tapestry, behind which a cat was hiding.

It's the statesman, not the conquering hero, who has a cat. Thomas Jefferson was fond of cats. Winston Churchill's ginger tomcat sat in on cabinet meetings, and the Prime Minister insisted on personally carrying him to the shelter during the London blitz. Louis XV's big white cat was the first visitor in his bedroom every morning. Queen Victoria's White Heather became a well-known personage, and Abraham Lincoln rescued three young cats he found half frozen in General Grant's camp.

Those who observe rather than control are the natural companions of the cat. Charles Darwin, Victor Hugo, Honoré de Balzac, Samuel Johnson, Montaigne, Thoreau, Matthew Arnold, Petrarch, Verlaine, Wordsworth, Sir Isaac Newton, and Sir Walter Scott loved cats. Henry James wrote with a cat on his shoulder. A catless writer is almost inconceivable; even Ernest Hemingway, manly follower of the hunting trophy and the bullfight, lived waist-deep in cats. It's a perverse taste, really, since it would be easier to write with a herd of buffalo in the room than even one cat; they make nests in the notes and bite the end of the pen and walk on the typewriter keys.

Mohammed had a cat named Muezza, which means "fairest and gentlest," and as we all know he cut off the sleeve of his robe where she was sleeping rather than disturb her. Jean Cocteau said the cat was the soul of his home. Alexandre Dumas said, "The cat, an aristocrat, merits our esteem, while the dog is only a scurvy type who got his position by low flattery." Mark Twain wrote, "A home without a cat, and a well-fed, well-petted, and properly revered cat, may be a perfect home, perhaps, but how can it prove title?"

Revered, yes. Revering a cat is by far the easiest way to get along with it on a day-to-day basis. You do not order a cat around, as this has no discernible effect and makes you feel like a fool, like Canute shouting at the tides. You respect a cat as an honored guest. This makes the least amount of work and frustration for you and minimizes stress in the relationship. The lazier you are about disciplining your cat and trying to impose your will on its ways, the happier you both will be.

It is the nature of a cat to do as it pleases. In the days before we met each other, the cat made up its own mind and took orders from no one, and obedience was never built into it. Many of the books on cat-keeping find this alarming, and warn us that a cat that gets its own way will grow up spoiled and disagreeable.

Certainly some cats, like some people, are disagreeable, but not because they're spoiled. I know a woman with a cat that bites her savagely if she infringes on its space or sleeps on the wrong side of the bed or breaks its rules, which it keeps changing. This is just not a nice cat. It may not have all its marbles. Any attempt at discipline might turn it totally savage, and I would give it away to my worst enemy and get a better cat. There are too many deserving kittens in need of homes to waste food and shelter on a monster. On the other hand, she's had this cat for many years and it's been biting her all along, so maybe they've worked out some sort of neurotic symbiosis; maybe we get the cats we want.

There are various books on the subject of "training" cats, and if you read too many you get the unsettling feeling that the authors have never laid eyes on a cat and are making the whole thing up, or else don't recognize a cat when they see one and are actually working with a kind of horizontal monkey or meowing dog. One book describes teaching a cat to roll over on command by harnessing it with a leash to a hook on the wall and pulling until the cat is dragged over onto its side, repeating the words "roll over" all the while. After an unspecified interval, the book claims, the cat will roll over when told to do so, instead of laying back its ears and leaving the room, and the house if possible, with all deliberate speed. This is clearly not a real cat of which he speaks. It may look like a cat to him, but closer inspection will reveal the slot where you push in two C batteries.

By and large, people who enjoy teaching animals to roll over will find themselves happier with a dog. Once, though, there was an Englishman named Leoni Clarke who made quite a good thing from a troupe of fifty performing cats. They walked across the stage on tightropes, stepping carefully over arrangements of mice, rats, and canaries, and they jumped through flaming hoops and parachuted down from the ceiling. Clarke billed himself as "The King of the Cats," and he must certainly have had some peculiar rapport with them. Perhaps he'd cracked the language barrier. It doesn't happen often.

There's a kind of elegance and poetry to the trained horse or dog, the Lippizaner and the working sheepdog, and the relationship between horse and rider, dog and shepherd, is enhanced until it glows, and illuminates the animals' lives by realizing their natural talents in a higher form. This simply isn't true for cats. We do not train a cat in anything that is useful to us or natural to the cat; you don't teach a cat to catch mice any more than you teach a hen to lay eggs. Teaching the useless and unnatural isn't training, it's pure trickery, and despicable in a way. Mr. Leoni's cats weren't herding sheep or carrying riders, they were entertaining paying customers with purposeless and undignified antics, and this is an unpleasant way to use an animal.

If we are to be friends with a cat, we must treat it with an egalitarian courtesy inappropriate for the dog and the horse, and make room in our lives for what is natural to the cats'.

Philosophical exception could be made for showing the cat how to use the toilet instead of the litter box, since it's useful to us and no more unnatural than using a litter box instead of a flower bed. Instructions are available, and several cats, all of them Siamese, turn up in the literature as having figured it out for themselves, presumably by imitation, which is much the easiest way to teach things to a cat. To explain the matter to the cat, first you put the litter box beside the toilet for a week so the cat gets used to the area. Then you start slipping things under the box to raise it an inch or so at a time, until it's on a level with the toilet seat. Now you replace it with a box designed to clip underneath the toilet seat; nobody says where to find such a thing, and I suppose you have to crate it yourself. Obviously, you have to leave it in place there, since cats take care of these matters on erratic schedules of their own. The books don't say what the humans are using in the meantime or how to explain it to visitors. Anyway, once the cat is using this device regularly you replace the box with one-inch wire mesh, to keep the cat from falling in. No cat likes to crouch on one-inch wire mesh, so it crouches, they say, on the toilet seat instead. Remove mesh. Mission accomplished.

I think it's on the last step that I'd lose my own cats; they would simply find it uncongenial and use the floor or the bathtub instead. Also they're in the habit of drinking from the toilet, and the dual-purpose aspect would be abhorrent to any right-thinking animal. But who knows? It might appeal to some, and certainly it's a swell conversation piece, and most cats would enjoy the cries of surprise and admiration from passersby.

The really basic book on educating cats begin with teaching him to use the litter box itself (hold his paw and make scratching motions in the litter; lock him in the room with the box), but I've never had to do that, merely show him where the thing is located, as one would with any guest. His mother taught him.

Most of the books say that a cat should know its name and come when called, and that would indeed be convenient. Kittens, unless they're very busy, come when their mother calls, especially if they're hungry, but then a hungry cat comes even when it isn't called. If you have nothing to offer that interests it, it doesn't, but this doesn't mean it doesn't know who it is.

I walk into a room where three cats are sleeping and speak the name of one, and it opens its eyes. It doesn't jump to attention, exactly, but it opens its eyes, cross at being waked for nothing.

We "train" it to know its name by using its name when we speak to it, especially while opening a can of cat food. Committed dog people will insist that unless it comes running when we say, "Charles, come here," then it can't actually *know* its name, but that is the way committed dog people think, or "think," confusing obedience with understanding.

Sometimes a name for a cat will spring to mind at once and stick with the cat forever; sometimes you can't decide, or the family disagrees and everyone calls it by a different name; sometimes you pick a name that sounds good at the moment but somehow slips off the cat later and falls into disuse, leaving it to go through life as The Siamese or The Black Cat. Children are easier, as we have to keep filling out tax forms and applications and documents with their names, and even if we're dissatisfied it's too late from day one.

From the cat's point of view, strong vowels are useful. It's a mistake to have Morgan and Corvo in the same house here; while they can distinguish between them, they both look up at the "or" sound. I'm trying to call the black kitten Spider, which won't fit her if she fills out later, but we need the long "i" sound in a house full of soft-vowel cats. This is no reflection on the cats' powers of discrimination. English is not their native tongue; even those of us who have studied a bit of French and can read it printed down may have trouble sorting out the Parisian taxi driver's opinions from his flow of sounds.

They know their names. They do not come when called. Cats are not just not obedient, they are actively disobedient. Gillette Grilhé, in *The Cat and Man*, says, "His pride forbids him to obey, or—if he does—he will do so only when a sufficient amount of time has passed after the order to make the full weight of his disdain felt, reacting only as a gesture of condescension."

Happily, by reason of its intelligence, modest size, delicate and cleanly habits, and general goodwill the cat may be considered to come preassembled and ready for use, naturally adapted, all uneducated as it is, for life in the homes of man.

Except for one small matter.

Some people care more than others about their furniture. Some have valuable and elegant couches, some are content with the effluent of attics, but nobody really wants to live among furnishings with woolly gray stuffing leaking from the sides and backs. It looks slovenly.

Cats scratch to hone their claws and keep them clean and exercise their backs and legs and mark their territories, and for various other reasons cited by the authorities, and because they like to. The books tell you to get a scratching post. It should be solidly based so as not to fall on the cat, and tall enough so he can stretch up full length to attack it. If you make it yourself and cover it with carpeting, glue the carpeting on inside out, with the tough, coarse backing material on the business side. Put some catnip inside it.

The authorities insist that the cat will gladly use the post instead of the armchair. Not just when he's passing by, but always. This has not been my experience, but then, as previously noted, the authorities have some strangely docile cats.

In spite of their confidence in the post, the books include methods to make your cat stop using the furniture anyway, such as crying "No!" and clapping your hands or swatting the couch with a rolled magazine to make a loud noise, which will frighten the cat away.

Once, maybe. The second time, a cat of any spirit will enjoy the fuss, and pin its ears back and scratch harder, watching for your reaction. Cats feeling bored, neglected, or ignored will head for the couch just to stir up some action and get some attention. Many cats, especially Siamese, rather enjoy being beaten a bit, and will scratch anything they can get their claws into to achieve this pleasure. Cats who don't want to get hit will scratch only until you drop what you're doing and hasten across the room with your hand raised, and then spring away just as the blow is falling to slip under the couch or up onto the curtain rod, out of reach. In the cats' eyes, it's the world's finest game.

You can spray a cat with a plant mister; this, too, comes highly recommended. By the second try my cats had figured out to the microsecond how long it takes to find the plant mister and pump it up to working capacity, and for the cat to be gone from the target area before the spray lands. The couch got wet, the cat stayed dry and hugely entertained.

In *The Siamese Cat*, Phyllis Lauder recommends growling at the cat the way its mother would if she were displeased with it. I tried this just once, and the cat seemed so confused and upset, and avoided me so nervously for days afterward, that I must have gotten the intonation wrong, or said something I didn't really mean. It's unwise to try to swear in unknown tongues.

One problem with all these methods is that they involve quitting your job and staying awake and in the living room twenty-four hours a day. Leave, and all bets are off.

There are products on the market, said to be feline repellents, for spraying on the furniture. My cats seemed not to notice them, but they made my guests sneeze uncontrollably.

The claws of an indoor cat grow out into a long curve like a miniature upholstery needle, ideal for slipping under threads; clipped claws do less damage. Some books recommend having your vet do this, but it isn't really that delicate a matter. You buy a clipper designed for the purpose, and do it in stages. Press on the paw pad to shoot the claw out of its sheath, and cut only the curved part, not the thin red line above it that hurts and bleeds. A cat that's fond of you will let you do three or four claws before he gets bored and leaves. Do the rest another time.

Or you can decide that by the time the couch starts to unravel you'll be tired of the blue velvet anyway, and it will do you and the living room a world of good to have it re-covered.

Or you can get different furniture. Some cats won't claw leather. A tight fabric like chintz doesn't unravel like wool, or offer a good hold. The modern unstructured things that are basically piles of pillows feel unstable to a cat, as if they might fall on his head, as well they might.

Or you can get the cat declawed.

Elizabeth Keifer in *Wholly Cats* writes that her veterinarian heartily approves of declawing, which, he says, gives neither pain nor psychic distress. Indeed, the cat never misses its claws at all, and its pads, he says, become so callused afterward that it has no trouble climbing trees.

He doesn't explain why the pads should get callused; a cat's claws are retractable, and the cat walks on the same pads before and after the operation. Nor does he explain how to climb a tree with callused pads. Would he care to put on some stout hard-surfaced mittens and scramble up to demonstrate?

A friend of mine had a little black cat named Siam and needed to leave it for the summer with her parents, but they insisted on having it declawed first, front and back, perhaps with visions of its standing on its head to slice upholstery from the rear. The next time I saw my friend, her parents, alas, were still unsatisfied. Siam cried night and day and kept them awake; she bit and chewed frantically at her paws so they didn't heal, and everywhere she went she left little rosebuds of blood on the precious upholstery and rugs.

Patricia P. Widmer, in *Pat Widmer's Cat Book*, recommends, almost insists on, declawing as a basic routine procedure like neutering, adding parenthetically that her cats are somehow managing to destroy her furniture anyway, but that fore-and-aft declawing is necessary to keep the cat from scratching people. I'm not sure I'd want to keep a cat that wanted in its heart to scratch me, front claws or back. Widmer doesn't mention trees, but she seems to live in

Manhattan and probably, like most New Yorkers, finds it hard to entertain the possibility of intelligent life elsewhere.

Dr. Susan McDonough, vet of final authority, says the world is full of cats kept locked away from normal life in kitchens or basements or bedrooms out of deference to the living room furniture, and claws are a reasonable price to pay for release.

My Persian Barney has been declawed. A cattery stud for his first ten years, he lost his claws when the cattery closed and the owner planned to take him to an apartment full of new chairs and couches. On an impulse, she gave him to me instead.

We lived in the city together and he learned a whole world of new things, refuting the scholarly theory that cats can learn new things during only a few brief months in their first year. He rejoiced in his retirement, and in having a person of his own.

After a couple of years, life being unpredictable, we found ourselves in the country instead. In the new place there was another cat, and Barney watched Sadie, and learned from her to sit on laps and ask for tidbits from the table.

Outdoors, for a clawless cat, was dangerous, so I kept him company on small excursions to the back porch. One day we sat there and watched Sadie climb up the willow tree, sit on a branch for a while, and climb back down.

Barney trembled all over. Racial memory sprang to life in this twelve-year-old cat who had never in his life before seen a tree up close. He whisked down the porch steps and trotted across the lawn with his tail on high and fluttering like a helmet plume. He put his paws on the tree and gave a little spring.

Using his clawed back feet for push, he got about three feet up before he toppled and fell over on his back on the ground; I heard the thump.

He wasn't hurt, but the cat that came back across the lawn was a different cat, and smaller than the one who had rushed to climb a tree at his ancestors' bidding, and his tail dragged in the grass.

Claws are central to a cat, to his ego, his sense of himself and his competence in the world. He sees himself as a creature with claws; they're as much a part of his inner image as arms are to us. When he raises a warning paw to an adversary, claws are what he means; when he signs a tree by scratching it, he was there, he left his mark; when he hooks open a cupboard door he is master of his world. He's a small animal, as predators go: claws are his stature in his mind's eye.

Oh, well. It's a fairly simple operation, and routinely performed now by all veterinarians, even those who hate it.

Tidy people make another problem for themselves from the matter of cats getting up onto tables and kitchen counters. The easiest way to deal with this is to tell ourselves the cat washes itself as diligently as we wash the table, and then throw it off only when we need the space for our own purposes. Perhaps our mothers won't agree, and it may not even be true, but it's certainly convenient to believe, and we aren't the first to hold a conviction from convenience.

My own cats sit on the dinner table, which I use—or try to use, among the cats—more for working than for dinner anyway, and when I bring out the plates and forks they get down, grumbling. Even cats who customarily sit on the table and watch while their person dines alone seems to realize that company alters the case. Or else company crowds the table unacceptably, or else they just don't like the company. In France, the cats of many famous statesmen and literary luminaries have always been welcome on the table, some of them with places regularly set for them. Germs are not a French obsession.

The uncharitable tell us that cats get up on counters because they want to steal food, but a properly treated cat who is fond of its people isn't anxious to steal their food. A purely functional cat, barely on speaking terms with its people and scrambling for enough to eat, might feel all food is fair game, but a personal cat will usually leave your chicken for you and wait by its dish. A cat knows the uses of food: when I tried to introduce a kitten into Blueberry's household she tried to starve him right back out again. A naturally dainty and desultory eater, she took to wolfing her dinner and then shoving the kitten aside and eating his too. She was going to get rid of that kitten if it choked her; as one's parents used to say, "If you don't feed it, dear, it won't hang around." What happy cat wants to starve out its people?

As the feline narrator of Paul Gallico's *The Silent Meow* says, "Stealing is for dogs. We are above it."

Exception must be made for cats that have conceived an unreasonable passion for food not on the ordinary menu. Jenny stole hot biscuits; Mai Tai snatched mushrooms from the refrigerator; Shibui will grab an ear of corn even from the diner's hand. The new black cat is frantic for pistachio nuts and French bread. Colette's mother's Long-Cat raided the garden for strawberries, asparagus, and melons, which last he slashed open with his claws. The literature also mentioned freshly ground coffee, olives, broccoli, grape jelly, and cinnamon Danish. Probably these exotic items aren't considered nourishment in the ordinary sense, and a cat that will steal our olives wouldn't steal our steak, or our mouse.

Why, then, if not to steal food, would a cat go up on the counter? Why did George Mallory try to go up on Mount Everest, which was quite a lot more trouble? Because it is there. Because of the view from the kitchen window. To lick the drips from the tap in the sink. To try to pry open the cupboards and see what's inside them, maybe to squeeze in among the glassware. Or, on a rainy day, to look for small objects to knock off onto the floor and see if they roll. And because it is in the nature of the cat to get up on things. Cats enjoy height. It makes them feel safer from nonclimbing things, and superior, and they can see farther. If our eyes were only six inches from ground level, we'd want to get up on something, too.

If we have a decent sort of cat to begin with, and have

always treated it courteously, and aren't cursed with meddling, bullying natures, it's a pleasure to let it do as it pleases. With children, this would be wicked and irresponsible, so raising children involves a lot of effort and friction. They need to be taught how to tie their shoes and multiply fractions, they need to be punished for pocketing candy in the grocery store, they need to be washed and combed and forced to clean up their rooms and say please and thank you.

A cat is our relief and reward.

4

Cats With People

It's part of the great body of cat lore that cats like their homes more than they like their people. If we move and take our cat long with us, tradition holds that its paws must be buttered to keep it from going back to the old place; the cat licks the butter off and decides to stay, perhaps because nobody ever buttered its paws in the old place.

The purely utilitarian cat, kept for reasons other than personal, might well feel more attached to place than to family, and find familiar faces and voices a poor substitute for familiar hunting grounds, but mostly a personal cat makes do with wherever its person takes it.

I move a lot, and no cat of mine ever suggested going back. They inspect the new quarters warily, checking baseboards and marking the edges of doors with their cheeks, and then curl up in their accustomed places on the accustomed furniture. Still, Sidney, in the move before last, was disappointed in the outside of the new house. It was in no way equal to the old outside; it had streets and cars instead of woods and fields, and he asked to have the door opened twenty times a day for weeks, and looked out, and then up at me, hoping that presently I would surround the new in with the old out. The others clearly understood that new houses mean new yards, but Sidney kept waiting and asking. With such a confused notion of place, it's doubtful he could ever find his way back home or much of anywhere.

Some cats do find their way. They do this by means that are totally mysterious and clearly superhuman, and consequently pretty annoying. Salmon and hummingbirds find their way too, but they're retracing, in the company of other salmon and hummingbirds, a journey they've made before under their own powers. A cat that was taken away by car or plane, locked up in a carrying case, can make its own way back again if it wants to badly enough, sometimes dying of exhaustion shortly after arrival. We don't know how it's done. The *Encyclopedia Britannica*, which has some curious notions about cats, thinks it's done by purring; a cat's purr, which has "no specific emotional connotations ... seems merely to be a homing device." They don't explain how it works, though, nor why a cat half asleep in its own living room would need a homing device. The *Britannica* may have cats confused with bats, who use a kind of sonar to find their way around.

Another theory holds that it's done by the position of the sun in relation to the exact time, which sounds more reasonable, especially if the differential is east-west and not north-south, and the cat is wearing a really accurate watch.

An investigator anesthetized a quantity of cats and put them in a car and drove them, completely unconscious, far away and dumped them; when they woke up they all went back home. Another investigator, however, proved they don't do any such thing. Under the auspices of Yale University, Donald Keith Adams conducted a series of experiments on eighteen cats that were kept, when not being investigated, in a bare stable and fed on a paste made principally of flour and water and alfalfa meal. He took one of them, in a box, two and a half miles from the laboratory and turned it loose to see if it could find its way back. The cat inspected the immediate area for a few minutes, and then moved quickly and purposefully off in a direction at right angles to the correct one and was never seen again. Some homes are hardly worth finding.

Every cat person knows a tale of a returning cat. Friends of mine were in a car accident while driving back from the New Jersey shore with their cat, and in the ensuing confusion the cat escaped into the woods; the people were treated for minor injuries and went sadly home, catless. Some weeks later the cat appeared on their doorstep on the far side of Philadelphia.

Philadelphia is a long, dreary, dangerous city to trek through on foot, and the bridges over the Delaware River from New Jersey are few and far apart; how would a cat, or even a person without maps or signs, know which roads led to bridges? How would it have the courage to cross those roaring vibrating metal spans? For how many days did it crouch in the weeds and stare at that rumbling high horror before setting foot on it? Or could it, maybe, swim? Cats are fair swimmers, but the Delaware there is a mighty stretch, open to international shipping, and poisonously filthy, full of rushing flotsam, sewage, oil slicks.

However many times we hear the stories, there's something moving about them. Even for a human on wheels, speaking the language and armed with street maps, it's not a light journey, along those highways and across that river and through that city; what a thing to require of a small speechless battered creature, thrown from a wrecked car.

And, of course, how did it know the way?

The unpalatable truth is that cats have ways of locating things that we can no more imagine than we can imagine inhabitants of another planet breathing methane gas. We're limited by our personal experience, whatever our pretensions to abstract conception.

At a cat show recently, two Siamese kittens escaped from their cage and vanished completely; the doors were locked and the building searched; no kittens. Some time later they were found out in the parking lot sitting on the roof of their own car, waiting. As a person who has more than once climbed into the driver's seat of a car like my own and tried futilely to turn my key in the ignition, a person who has many times, with eyes places far above tire level and a rudimentary knowledge of automotive makes and models, searched vainly for my car in a parking lot, I find this just as mysterious as homing. It seems to be a sense of the uniqueness of a thing, so that there can be only one right car, only one right road, and these right things call to the cat, and are not to be confused with other, identical, cars and roads. The sense works in unfathomable ways, and fails just as unfathomably: a cat who has seen your briefcase a hundred times in your hand or in the closet may be terrified of it on the living room floor, fluff up its tail, approach it cautiously, ready to turn and flee, and then, inches away, recognize it and feel a perfect fool and have to sit down and wash or pretend to be interested in something else across the room.

How can a creature who can find its own car in a lot or its own home across three states fail to recognize a brief-case in the wrong place? We'll never know. We see things, not as themselves, but as members of classes and catego-ries, and that leads us to use different equipment. Maybe we never had the sense of things from the beginning, or maybe we've been relying too long on crutches like reason and maps.

If stories about homing cats rouse the sympathies, and the impulse to reach a hand across time and space to help, stories of psi trailing simply make us nervous.

Psi trailing is the scientific name for the unscientific act of finding people who went away into the unknown.

Friends of my family gave their cat to a kind neighbor in Washington, D.C., when they moved to Ohio. The cat, who has never been out of Washington before, took five months to find them. The man of the family still staunchly insists that it can't be the same cat, only an identical cat with iden-tical habits that came to their door clamoring to be let in, emaciated and with serious clinical evidence of hard travel-ing, five months after their own cat had vanished from her new home. I know how he feels. Veterinary and dental ev-idence be damned; things like that can get on your nerves.

Dr. J. B. Rhine, former director of the famous Parapsychology Laboratory at Duke University, investigated and substantiated some of these stories. In two of the best-documented cases, a veterinarian's cat found him in California after he'd moved there and left it behind in New York, and a part Persian named Sugar took fourteen months to find her family's new home in Oklahoma after they'd left her in California; small but distinctive bone deformities clinched both identifications.

Cats, says Konrad Lorenz, will never love you the way a dog does, but what unimaginable longing could force a cat out of a comfortable home to risk its life on such a desperate trip? And what molecular evidence has our passage left in the air to be followed; what recognizable tracks did our tires leave on I-95? What unique vibrations are we emitting from our new house two thousand miles away?

Best not to think about it.

And on the other hand, George the First quite deliberately left his home and family and moved to another house two blocks away. Our house was full of noise and small children; he put up with us for several years and then disappeared. He was searched for and mourned, and then months later my mother saw him, sitting on his new front porch looking sleek. "George!" she cried, outraged. He answered at once, and trotted over to rub her ankles and be patted and speak in his distinctive polysyllabic voice, and then he went back up his front steps and settled down again. The house looked quiet and comfortable and there was no evidence of children.

In the matter of homes, a cat can decide to better itself.

Caroline bettered herself.

Caroline was born in a part of the world where the dogs are treated more tenderly than the children and live in pampered luxury, while the cats live outside and remain nameless. Since no cat is ever vaccinated, vast numbers of them die of enteritis in infancy; but since no cat is ever neutered, there are always more. They're attached to the property in the same sense as the birds at the bird feeder, and to wonder about the quality of their lives would be considered sentimental; to keep one as a household pet is a sign of senility. They are wild and shy, but they stay where they are, half fed, unpetted, untreated for wounds or parasites or diseases; it takes an exceptional cat to dream of something better without evidence that it exists.

The striking thing about Caroline's arrival was that she seemed to know exactly what she was doing as she came across the yard toward the house; she moved like a cat coming home in time for dinner. She seemed, in retrospect, like some healthy, hopeful, immigrant girl approaching Ellis Island with a shabby traveling bag and a determined light in her eye. She didn't pause or detour to inspect the trees and rocks; she headed straight for the door, and I opened it, and she came in. I had the uneasy feeling that I must have invited her somehow, or hired her, and forgotten, and here she was at the appointed hour.

Only the sudden appearance of our dog, Vicky, confused her, and she fluffed up and jumped onto the mantelpiece; apparently she'd seen the whole place clearly in her mind except for the dog. After watching closely for a while, she saw that the resident cats ignored the dog, so she jumped back down and went over to Vicky and with the prettiest possible gesture walked under her chin, arching her back against it, as a sign of friendship and perhaps apology.

The other cats accepted her as if they'd known for weeks that she was coming. She had naturally sweet manners; perhaps intercat civility is essential in the marginal world she came from, or life would have been chaos. She never forgot the little niceties, like the lick that asks permission to join another cat in its patch of sunshine. She was also the only grateful cat I've ever known, and in foul weather sat for hours on the windowsill and looked out, and then turned and looked in, surveying the warm room, the soft furniture, the cat dishes on the kitchen floor, and then looked at me and half closed her eyes and flexed her paws.

Because of a kind of modesty in her she never became a major cat around the house; she wasn't shy, but she never pushed her way into people's affections or laps and seemed always to remember that the others were there first. And maybe she'd accomplished what she set out to do. Maybe the comfortable home was what she'd come to find, and affection was beyond the scope of her plans.

What brought her, my immigrant girl? Did she see it all in a dream and go out and follow it, like a biblical figure obeying the voice of the Lord? How did George find the childless house on Primrose Street? It's unlikely he went there begging for food; he was indecently well fed. What brings cats to my sister's sanctuary; what changed Boston Blackie's mind? Why did Rose, a city stray, sit for three months on Patti's windowsill and stare compellingly in at her until finally, tired of hiding from her, Patti, who had never liked cats, let her in? Rose was right, and it turned out to be the perfect home, but how did she know this before Patti herself knew? How did Gloria, another city stray, know the exact moment when Elaine and Vic began recovering from the death of Jemima, and arrive to climb screaming insistently up the back door? Is it possible that cats, so long revered as the demigods and protective spirits of the domestic hearth, can foresee a new home as well as locate an old one?

It might be.

Certainly cats, or some cats at least, have a strong sense of the home as place, as walls enclosing something more than furniture and people. In the country the Siamese Corvo went abroad to look into other people's houses. He sat on the windowsill or perched on a low branch and looked in the window, and the people, going about their business, ironing clothes, playing Scrabble, fidgeting under his scrutiny. He didn't want to go inside, or to be petted or fed. With miles of woods and hunting grounds at his disposal, he wanted to look into a human house instead, and absorb the sense of it. Barney, when we lived in an apartment, visited the other apartments in the building. He wasn't visiting the people, as a dog might; he took an interest in the apartments for their own sake, scarcely glanced at the residents, and walked around in their rooms like a prospective lessee. Is there more under our roofs than we know?

Some cats people their own places with imaginary spirits. Sidney has for weeks now been very angry with the wall forming the side of the staircase at the back of the living room. Not the whole wall, but a section about a third of the way along it. He sits glaring furiously at it. He can't pass by it without a malevolent glance, and sometimes he attacks it and tries to rend its bland unmarked surface with his claws. My cousin's cats, Thing One and Thing Two, spent a substantial part of their lives peering nearsightedly at an area just above the baseboard of the wall in the hall, an occupation they seemed to find endlessly satisfying, like reading a good book. Colette, in *The Cat*, speaks of "the fixed attention she gave to things swimming about in the air in front of her eyes ... 'What is that cat staring at? Tell me. There's nothing where she's looking,' 'Nothing ... for us.' "

In *The Good Cat Book* Mordecai Siegal says cats stare at the wall so people can make fools of themselves trying to figure out why.

Efforts at scientific thought are caught in a bind here. We can't very well allow ourselves to believe in actual invisible spirits in the home, nor can we allow a cat a human imagination, so we're left believing that some cats, normal in all other respects, are subjected to psychotic delusions that manifest themselves only inside the cats' own homes. Even at that, it's a strain to allow something so presumably simple as a cat something as sophisticated as a delusion. A delusion of *what*, for heaven's sake? What shape does it take for them, what does it mean? Why are some delusions enraging and others merely interesting? Is it a form of religion? A chemical imbalance in the brain? How is it related to the physical house itself, so that a cat with a delusion in one house has none when it moves to another, and if it is house-connected, is it part of what calls a cat home across long distances?

And can a bored cat summon up a delusion for entertainment, the way we turn on the television? Should we replace this possibly unwholesome recreation with real television?

Some cats, I'm told, watch a lot of it. Maybe they have larger screens and better reception than my cats do, or maybe, like our children, they find it easier than summoning genies out of the imagination. It would be interesting to know if they have an preferences in programs, if the content makes any difference to them. Does what a cat sees on television make any narrative sense to it? Most cats recognize their reflections in the mirror as being cats, so presumably people on television look like people, but would they understand, for instance, a chase?

Barney once watched an entire program about caribou. It was one of those hypnotically peaceful public broadcast programs that all seem to be about a hundred years in the day of a sandhill crane, only these were caribou. Caribou walking back and forth, moulting and migrating, eating and giving birth, accompanied by the singsong drone of narration, and Barney watched each caribou's every step, utterly absorbed, only his eyes moving as it crossed the screen. When it was over he got down off the table and went out to the kitchen to check his dish.

He has never watched anything since, or shown the slightest interest in subsequent nature programs.

Why caribou?

Morgan also watched them once. This program was about birds, a twittering flock of them, and she watched until they all flew upward and vanished from the screen. She raised her head and looked up over the television, and then turned to inspect all the corners of the ceiling; no birds. She was displeased: not real birds at all, then, but a trick, a joke to play on cats. She left the room and has never again even glanced at the television; if she sits on my lap while I'm watching, she closes her eyes. She seems to me an earthy, sensible, pragmatic sort of cat, and has no delusions and no use for unreal birds.

The ways in which they share our lives and occupations and accommodate themselves to our households vary from cat to cat. Some cats listen to music, or to certain kinds of music, with every sign of enjoyment. Some are indifferent to it and some, like my Blueberry, find it all excruciatingly painful. Morgan hates guitars. My aunt had a cat named Simke who hated Caruso. She ignored all other vocalists, but Caruso's opening notes sent her yowling across the room, throwing herself against the door to get out. In *Are Cats People?* Paul Corey mentions playing a Caruso record that always brought a neighbor's cow galloping across the field to lean over the fence and moo. Perhaps investigators could spend a couple of grants analysing Enrico's vibrations.

Sidney, though not intelligent, is musical. A lot of his vocal expressions seem to be musical in intent if not in effect, and he used to play the piano. He played in the classical kitten-on-the-keys fashion, by walking on it, but he stepped thoughtfully, and paused, and sometimes crouched to produce chords with his haunches, all with deliberation and obvious enjoyment. He's an insomniac, and from time to time I woke up in the dark hours at four in the morning to the unsettling notes of a piano in the empty living room below.

Then one day Sidney watched my husband playing. He sat on the floor and stared and stared, apparently never having noticed before: the man sat on the piano stool and used only his two hands. When my husband vacated the stool, Sidney hopped up onto it. He sat and looked at the keys. He lifted a front paw and reached out tentatively and touched one. Nothing happened. Presently he got down and went away, and never again went anywhere near the piano.

Sidney has always shown uncatlike signs of feeling inferior to people, or that people were somehow doing things the right way and cats the wrong way. At dinner he sits on the extra chair, not on the table, and watches the people eat. When he accepts a tidbit, instead of putting his face down and eating it cat-fashion, he hooks at it a while with his paw, as if wishing he could use a knife and fork on it, correctly. It seems fair to suppose he felt that my husband was playing the piano correctly, and since as a cat he couldn't do it that way, then he wouldn't do it at all. I don't think he envied the actual sounds produced—he'd always seemed pleased with his own efforts. It was only the method he couldn't master.

Cats give up quickly. It is not in the nature of the cat to struggle for accomplishment against heavy odds. A cat that has tried a difficult jump and fallen, or failed to make sense of television, or to play the piano properly, will not persevere. It will turn its attention elsewhere. Cats dislike failure, especially in public, and prefer doing the things they're good at and dealing with things they understand; the incomprehensible they simply turn their backs on, and wash. Perhaps the human race would be in more peaceful circumstances today if we weren't so proud of our passion for solving riddles and conquering obstacles.

There are usually enough things to do that a cat is good at to keep it busy, and many more things for two cats. If we keep our cat closed in, in house or apartment, and especially if we're often away, it's only humane to have two or more to ward off boredom and loneliness and too much communing with the spirits of the wall. Two cats take up very little more room than one, and the games of two cats are more fun for humans as well as for cats.

To the restless, ambitious human mind the normal occupations of a house cat seem idle and frivolous. Except for persuading people to open doors and cans, they are not what career counselors call goal-oriented. They include lying in the sun, eating house plants, many of which are poisonous, squeezing into boxes too small for them so that folds of cat hang over the edges, looking out the window, rummaging in bureau drawers, and watching their humans.

How do we appear to our cats, that so many seem so interested in and even so deeply attached to their people? In *Cat Behavior*, Paul Leyhausen says that the cat's dependent life with people is a kind of extended kittenhood, so that it transfers its affection from its mother to us, and we stand to it in her place while it accepts our care, though from time to time it's seized by a fit of adulthood and asserts its independence. Living, in short, like a permanently thirteen-year-old human, an appalling thought. I've been pushing this theory around for a while, but I'm still not sure about it. It doesn't quite ring true; it's too easy. All right, once in a while a cat will behave like an adolescent person, but only under stress.

When I had pneumonia, Boy, the black supercat, the major cat of my life, spent his days and nights by my side, watching me. Then I went away, to the hospital, for ten days. There can be no connection in a cat's mind, unless just possibly death, between a person's illness and subsequent disappearance. For ten days he lived an apparently normal life in his own home among familiar things and people; he was fed regularly and ate his food. When I came home he refused to greet me or even meet my eyes. I reached down with an apologetic pat, and pulled back my hand: his fur was disgusting. He was filthy. He was so dirty he was almost sticky to the touch. Always a vain cat, he burnished his slick black coat till it flashed blue glints in the sunlight, but since my disappearance he obviously hadn't given even the most cursory lick. Now he walked a few feet away and sat down with his back to me. He was very angry, but I had finally come home, and he began to wash. He spent the remainder of the day washing; it was a long, disagreeable job—he was a perfect Augean stable of a cat; he even smelled bad, my flower-scented Boy—but when he was finished he glittered as before. He still didn't speak to me, though. It was days before he forgave me and things were the same between us.

That was adolescent of him, a thoroughly adolescent revenge, not washing because I'd abandoned him. But who among us, caught in a painful and incomprehensible position with no way to fight back, hasn't stooped to unworthy reactions at some time in our adult lives? Given the helplessness of their small size and limited communications with the masters of the house, a cat may be driven to expressions of frustration that seem childish to us. Childish and sometimes repulsive. Without a common language, a cat who must tell us something is limited to the use of its body and the functions thereof.

The most obvious form of expression it has is what I suppose I must call defecation. Cats invest heavy emotions in their toilet functions. A cat outdoors finding the right place to use, and using it, is a busy and seriously involved creature. Indoors, the litter pan is an important element in life. Sidney even has a special noise, or song, he makes when he's about to use it, and another, victorious song that means he's done so; sometimes he tears around the house afterward ruffling up the rugs with a wild light in his eyes.

In my unfeeling youth I kept a lone and lonely cat in my apartment and went off to work every day. Sometimes I went out after work and was gone all evening as well, and when I did this the cat would leave me a small pile on the floor directly beside the litter pan, no more than half an inch from it, to underline that this was no thoughtless accident but a deliberate message of anger and loneliness.

My grandmother's Siamese went further. My grandmother was old and ill, and a nurse-companion was hired to live with her. Nurse-companionship isn't a very desirable career, and the people who go in for it are not always the best and brightest. This woman was slovenly, cross, and disagreeable, and resented the extra work of feeding and opening doors for a cat. No one knows in what ways she revenged herself on the cat, but the cat retaliated with the only weapon she had to hand. She slipped into the room where the woman slept and left her weapon on the pillow, not once but several times. Maybe it was only simple vengeance; more likely she took it a step further and hoped that the woman, rather than sleep in a pile of feces, would simply go away.

She didn't, of course. Nurse-companions, even horrid ones, are hard to find, and it was the cat herself who went away to a shelter.

A cat who uses secret, hidden places as a toilet has some other and deeper problem, but a cat who leaves the matter in plain sight has something important to say. No matter how thoughtfully we care for it, there is always that element of helplessness in communication that forces the cat into infantile behavior, but I don't think we need to interpret this as a relationship of childish dependence.

In fact, it sometimes seems quite the opposite, and the cats, especially females, treat their humans with the worried protective bossiness of anxious mothers, and fret inordinately over illnesses or accidents. Blueberry used to try to rescue me from the bathtub, lest I drown. When my children were young, their cuts and scrapes and howls of pain drew cats of both sexes, distressed and fussing and interfering with the first aid. Many are the stories of cats watching tirelessly at sickbeds, of cats alerting their people to fires or choking babies, even of cats hunting and bringing back small game for people trapped or in wartime peril or famine: are these dependent children, or responsible adults in the family?

Few things about the cat can be exposed to the daylight of reason, least of all how it stands, in its own eyes, in its relationship to us.

Why do cats bring us things? Country dwellers are accustomed to the rows of corpses on the morning doorstep, mice and moles and the occasional bird or baby rabbit. People in apartments whose cats don't go out may wake up in the morning beside a row of small objects, socks and matchbooks and the like; a friend of mine woke up with a dead rat on her chest. My daughter's cat Hector, living illicitly in a college dormitory, foraged around and brought things back to her in her room, underwear and earrings and, once, a dollar bill. Blueberry, an apartment cat, never showed the least interest in hunting even when taken to the country, but she brought me a dead crow once, an enormous crow half again as big as the cat, struggling down the driveway and up the walk to lay it at my feet with every sign of pride. She didn't kill it, it had been shot by hunters, and I'm not sure whether I was supposed to think she did, or only be pleased because this is the kind of thing humans want.

They don't expect us to eat what they bring, apparently, any more than the gods of primitive religions are expected to actually eat the sacrificed sheep or bullock or virgin. Cats show no other sign of regarding us as gods, and religion, even primitive religion, is held to be one of the immovable barriers separating humanity from the lowly beast, but what *are* these offerings? I have heard of a cat, rescued in wintertime as a stray, who was deeply concerned with keeping warm. His house had a basement furnace that sent heat up through a floor grating, on which he luxuriated. When the furnace went off he anxiously rounded up all his toys and carried them to the grating and laid them out. A sacrifice? A trade? A bribe?

Sometimes there's a sexual element in the relationship, and cats attached to a human of the opposite sex will be sharply jealous of a spouse or lover. With Barney, in the beginning, the relationship was obviously sexual, but then, life as a cattery stud doesn't teach a cat much about other ways of feeling. From time to time he would scramble onto my back and try to hold me by the neck with his jaws, as he used to do with his Persian clients. He had strong feelings about me, and this was the only thing he knew to do about feelings. Later, after he'd had a chance to watch other cats with people, he learned the sadly limited repertoire at his disposal: the flexed paw, the purr, the stomach exposed for rubbing, the half-closed eyes. Dogs can show their devotion by a glad submission, but cats and people can only signal a little to each other across the gulf, like lovers in adjacent prisons.

Cats enjoy our company, compete for our attention, and often seem to love us deeply, and we don't know why; we don't even understand its simplest expression.

Take the matter of purring, a mystery so impenetrable that entire books are written about cats without mentioning it. We assume that purring means affection, but a number of authorities say no, and cite the fact that cats will purr when frightened. I don't think this reaction is all that common; in a long life among cats I've heard it only once, from a vet's examining table; I thought the cat had gone mad. Perhaps it was a plea for clemency. Perhaps it was a kind of hysteria; laughter in humans is supposed to mean pleasure, but a frightened human may laugh from pure nervousness.

How can we doubt, with the *Britannica*, that purring means what we think it means? Recently at the zoo I watched a pair of tigers in amorous dalliance; between matings the male threw himself down on his side with a thud and gazed at the female and purred until the sidewalk shook under my feet. An affectionate cat purrs when patted or spoken to by its human or nestled into a lap, and a cross cat will refuse to purr. Paul Gallico in *The Silent Meow* calls this The Withheld Purr, a useful form of communication. You speak kindly to the cat and rub gently under its jaw with your finger, and the cat should purr; you expect it to purr; you can almost hear it purr; but it doesn't. The silence bursts on you with its information: you have displeased this cat somehow.

From a scientific viewpoint the problem of the purr is that by the time the investigator gets inside to search out the mechanism the cat has stopped purring. The great naturalist Gilbert White said parts of its windpipe are "formed for sound." The *Encyclopedia Americana* offers two theories—vibrations of the false vocal chords that lie above the true ones, or of the hyoid apparatus, which are small bones between the skull and larynx. *The World Book Encyclopedia* leans toward a theory of blood vessels with vibrating walls inside the chest, while Elizabeth Keifer in *Wholly Cats* says it's made by vibrating the soft palate and resembles snoring in humans, which raises various questions, such as how they purr when awake and can they, unlike the rest of us, vibrate the soft palate at will? *Pat Widmer's Cat Book* makes the inarguable statement that "purring is a noise made by the cat while breathing." Therein lies the investigator's dilemma: a cat that stops breathing stops purring.

The most recent report, in *The Compendium on Continuing Education for Veterinary Medicine*, is that cats can control the air pressure through the glottis, the opening of the larynx, both inhaling and exhaling, as if we could produce a continuous "hummmm" sound breathing in as well as out. *Veterinary Aspects of Feline Behavior* says that kittens begin to purr at the age of two days, using the vibration to locate important landmarks like their mother, and then after their eyes open they extend the purr's purpose to include a call for food or attention. And public broadcast television says the purr, a consistent twenty-five vibrations per second, means the cat wants a contact to be continued: if you're holding me, go on holding me.

Don't stop. Don't leave.

We do leave, though. Perhaps so much fuss is made over the loyalty of dogs because we ourselves are capable of such treachery, and can terminate a relationship without a backward glance, breaking our contract with an animal whenever it seems convenient to do so. Many are the classified ads and notices on bulletin boards: "Free to good home; moving." From the frequency with which we abandon our friends you'd think a cat was more trouble to crate and transport than a breakfront full of grandmother's china. It's not likely we'll find a good home, not for a grown cat, and what, from its point of view, is a good home? Perhaps anywhere, any motel room, as long as we were there. Let's not be too easily satisfied with a roof and regular meals for our old companion; it may be we have broken his heart. When our own hearts are broken we can rationalize them whole again, or pull our pride over the wounds. A cat can't. He may go on living in the new home for many years, and listen for our voice and footstep every day of them.

We made a contract, and the fine print is in a language we can't read. There are connections here we don't know about, or how can a cat go find its person half a continent away? Honoré de Balzac's cat asked to go out every day in time to meet him coming home from work, but when the man silently changed his plans and wasn't coming home, the cat stayed curled in its chair and didn't bother to go out.

Of course it's also possible to have a cat around on a totally impersonal basis, to catch mice or decorate the living room sofa, as long as you're sure you both understand the terms.

Jane kept Esmeralda to catch mice. The two of them lived alone together in a big house on a windswept hill, and Jane complained often of loneliness, and invited me over. Esmeralda got to know me (I slipped her bits of cheese from the cocktail table; "Stop it," said Jane, "you're giving her ideas above her station") and the sound of my car, and always waited in the hall to greet me. The three of us sat in the living room, and Jane complained of loneliness.

"You have Esmeralda," I offered.

"Huh. Esmeralda."

At the sound of her name the cat gazed adoringly at Jane and flexed her paws deeply into the rug.

"She loves you," I said. "Look at her. She's asking to sit in your lap." Esmeralda reached out a polite paw and touched the couch by Jane's leg, asking.

"She does not love me. She only wants to sit in my lap so she can scratch me."

"*Scratch* you?"

Jane nodded emphatically. "That's what she wants to do. I let her sit in my lap just once, and she dug her claws right into my leg like a savage."

"Oh, Jane, she didn't mean it that way. It means love, and pleasure. It's because kittens do it to their mothers when they're nursing, kneading their paws like that."

"I'm sorry for their mothers, then. And if that's her idea of love, no thank you."

Esmeralda slitted her green eyes at Jane and purred hoarsely.

"Let her sit beside you, then. Invite her up."

Instead Jane scooped up the cat and carried her to the basement door. "She can stay down there. She's a useless cat and I've got a good mind to get rid of her. I got her to catch mice. The people said her mother was a great mouser, and does Esmeralda catch mice? Hell, no. She plays with them. She's made friends with them, I caught her sharing her food with them."

"What?"

"You heard me. I opened the basement door and there they were, there she was by her dish and there were two or three mice with her, and they ran away when they saw me. She was letting them eat out of her dish. I'd just like to give her back to those liars who gave her to me, it would serve them right."

The stairs down to the basement were steep and long, and Jane had a bad knee, but every day she carried Esmeralda's dinner dish down those stairs and set it next to the litter pan, an uncongenial arrangement to say the least, rather than share her big bright kitchen with a cat. Alone in her living room Jane watched television and complained of loneliness. Alone in the dark basement the cat, desperate, made friends with mice like prisoners in the dungeons of song.

"Damned useless cat." Jane slammed the basement door. "I expect she does it just to spite me, she knows I hate mice."

And so they lived together there for several years, woman and cat, until Jane died of the various complications of loneliness and relatives drove Esmeralda to the vet to be "put to sleep," as we like to call it.

If we don't expect to love a cat, we should be careful to find out what the cat expects. And if we don't plan on a personal relationship, we must at least arrange for it to have some company, some friendship. The cat goes hunting by itself, because that's the way a cat has to hunt, but it doesn't choose loneliness. It seems to contain great secret lakes and continents of generous affection, much of it, surprisingly, for us, and it shouldn't have to pass its days in such miserable solitude that it shares its food with mice.

5

Cats With Cats

Relations between cat and cat are as complex and stylized as Chinese ideographs. It's easier, really for cats to get along with people. Friendships between cats and people come naturally and are simple enough, sometimes dangerously simple, to establish. Just leave the door open a minute too long on a dark and catless night, then turn back into your house and it has a cat, like a puff of fog blown in, and it turns out you've met before in an earlier life. The cat was born knowing how to arch its back under your hand, and your hand knows how to smooth itself along the cat in a gesture clinically proven to soothe you both. The cat will settle down with its paws folded under its breast and accept you with its eyes, and be perfectly at ease in your presence. You are natural companions.

Getting along with other cats takes teaching. Cat manners and communication are taught positively by example and negatively by direct, sometimes very direct, instruction from any other cat close enough to aim a slap. Some of it come built into the cat; a kitten with a safe and happy mother never saw her fluff her tail and hiss, but surprise this infant in its box and it swells into a spitting pincushion. The smaller the kitten, the more thoroughly it can fluff itself to look bigger. A grown cat expands its tail and a ridge of fur along its arched back, turning sideways to the enemy to show the full effect, but the kitten bristles all over. You can say a lot with fur. Lions, instead of turning sideways, face the threat head-on to show the splendid intimidating mane and hide the absurdly unimposing leonine rear. Dogs' hackles are confined to the back of the neck and frontal spine, and raising them means the same thing. A friend of mine has a Rhodesian ridgeback whose hackles are permanently raised, stiff as a hairbrush even in her sleep, and this gets her in trouble, as if she were a human waving a loaded shotgun. On her most peaceful country strolls, farm dogs see her and react by either slinking away or taking up the challenge.

Tails communicate, too. They may possibly help a cat right itself in midair, but they aren't for balancing with; they're for conversation, like a dog's tail. The vertebrae of the cat, from skull to tail tip, are flexibly connected so the cat can contract and expand its length, curve its back upward as well as down, or ripple it along the spinal line, and my mother's cat Tadger can roll up his tail like a stuffed anchovy. The language of the tail raises questions about the tailless cats that turn up here and there through history; are they semimute in the cat world, or have they found another, invisible way to communicate, maybe with a wider range of scents?

A kitten running to greet its mother carries the tail straight up but relaxed at the end, so the tip flutters like a waved hand. In later life it will use this position to greet its human and to trot in to dinner. Put the dish on the floor, and if the food is acceptable the tail drops slowly until it lies straight out and flat on the floor, ready to be stepped on, while the cat eats. If the food is no good the tail drops only to half mast while the cat makes scratching motions on the floor around the dish, meaning that this smells so foul that it will bring enemies from far and wide unless we bury it, or, metaphorically, this shit belongs in the litter box. Some sources maintain that the cat is trying to bury it for safekeeping, to return for it later, but my cats never go back.

The fluffed tail held up stiff clear to the tip is a threat; up and arched forward it's defensive. Then there's the inverted U, an anxious sign seen in the pursued cat during a rough game of tag, and the fluffed inverted U, half offense, half defense.

These matters are pretty well standardized, though as usual with cats, not universal; I knew a pair of white cats who always carried their tails resting comfortably between their ears, and what other cats made of this unorthodoxy I can't imagine. Turkish Angoras do the same, and presumably understand each other.

Fur and tail combined with the hundred variations of body posture, of ears, whiskers, pupil dilation, and verbal comments make up an intercat vocabulary not demonstrably smaller than that of the average American high school student. Making friends is another matter.

Friendships between cat and cat are a luxury, born when the cat of civilization no longer needs solitary hunting grounds in order to survive. Cat friendships are a gift we can give them, a subsidiary of guaranteed meals and sexual cancellation.

Hunting animals are never automatically at ease with each other the way plant-eaters are. Cows in a field, antelope on the plain, finches in a flock, need each other deeply and mutely, and except for the squabbles of mating season draw great comfort from knowing there's another of the same kind around. They think communally, a single idea flowing like water through the group. On catching sight of a neighbor grazing nearby they don't need to have any special reaction or establish any specific relationship between themselves and this other; a cow is unsurprised to see another cow, and never has to ask if this cow is stronger or braver than she is, or is chewing a better bite of grass. Either there is grass to eat or there is no grass; one doesn't compete for grass.

Meat-eaters need more space, and their food comes singly, meal by meal. An eagle can't afford to ignore another eagle nesting next door, and a cat moving into the hunting grounds is a rival cat. Among cats every chance meeting is an encounter, and needs alert consideration; a cat pretending to ignore another cat is playacting. He looks at the sky, he licks a perfectly clean spot on his side, the feline equivalent of shoving your hands in your pockets and whistling. He yawns, and almost, but not quite, closes his eyes; let the other cat make a move and all the lights snap on at once.

Outdoors, cats have a home territory, to be defended, and beyond it a home range, an area full of special spots for hunting or resting or watching, all connected by invisible pathways, and this they'll share with other cats, avoiding direct encounter when they can. Bobcats in the wild cover extensive tracts of land, and a study showed that they all circled through the territory counterclockwise, so as not to bump into each other and have to make a scene. Domestic cats using the same range may work out a time-sharing schedule. Sometimes it's prearranged by time of day— morning cat, afternoon cat, evening cat—and sometimes they lay messages like the Occupied sign on a public toilet; the first cat into the field leaves scent markers on the path, and the next cat, sniffing, can tell whether they're fresh and he should turn aside and go a different way, or whether they're several hours old and their creator finished his hunting now and is out of the way.

Scent is sophisticated communication for cats. All of us, coming home, have been checked out by our cats and wondered if the cat may not know as much about where we've been as we do. Between cat and cat, smell is raised to an art form. Scent glands are stationed along the tail, on each side of the forehead, and on the lips and chin; a cat that rubs its face against you is marking you for its own. A possessive cat like Morgan marks everything she can reach, especially when it isn't hers; at my mother's house she claimed all the doorways and furniture and my mother as well, to the indignation of Mother's own cat. Even the pads of the feet leave messages, as the cat walks through the world like a graffiti artist leaving his name on bridges and buildings.

Most cat marks are subtle, and invisible to the human nose, but spraying is something else again, a gross message even humans can read, though all it means to us is "cat." Sniffing it, the cat opens its mouth in what looks to us like an expression of angry disgust, but what it's doing is opening an auxiliary nose. This is the "flehmen reaction," and it gets the smell's information to the ducts behind the upper incisors that channel it to the vomeronasal organ for decoding. Some researchers believe a cat may leave a record, not just of its presence, but of its age and sex and status, emotional state, readiness for love, and individual identity. As much, in short, as a human can pack into a personals ad, and far more likely to be true.

A leopard, most solitary of cats, adds a postscript; he sprays a tree and then stands on his hind legs and claws the bark as far up as he can reach, meaning, "Back off; an enormous cat with very sharp claws lives here."

Recent studies suggest that even we are more sensitive to smell than we realize. Maybe because we smelled so personally unpleasant for so much of our history we came to suppress olfactory information as both impolite and disgusting. Cats never smelled bad. They buried their excrement and cleaned their fur with a saliva that contains a cleansing and deodorizing agent, and left themselves open to the educational symphony of smell. Lend your cat carrier to someone else, and when it's brought back your cat can spend twenty minutes with it, learning who knows what richly detailed nuances about your friend's cat and its life and secret name. We'd consider it rude to sniff our friends for news, because until very recent times indeed one's friends didn't bear close sniffing; instead we stand well back and say, "How have you been? Are you feeling better? Are you happy?" and very likely get a lie in return. Cats can't lie to the noses of other cats.

Once full identification is made the cats decide, on the evidence, whether to fight, or threaten, or separate, or pursue the acquaintance.

In a large household, a colony really, the size of my sister's, there seem to be few close friendships or strong enmities, as if the sheer numbers re-created a solitary state; they are part of a whole, like soldiers in an army, and used to each other, but except in very cold weather they maintain air space in between. The disappearance of one or the arrival of another causes little comment. This seems sensible. Cats are not cattle, to huddle blankly together, and to have to take sharp emotional notice of so many others every day would be exhausting; easier to remain aloof.

After breakfast they fan out like the spokes of a wheel. Zachary goes down the driveway toward the woods, Flanagan through the neighbor's yard and around the north side of my house, Ferdie through the back hedge, Marzipan across the vegetable garden; their paths neither cross nor conflict. (Basil, having found his home, stays by it, pressed heavily against its wall to pin it down.) Indoors, no one has made an effort to stake out a particular chair or rug; presumably it would take so much defending there'd be no time for sleep. But outside there's space enough for each to have his own, established by custom and mutual consent rather than confrontation. It's recognized that these paths and areas are not property, to be defended, but rights-of-way only. It would be bad manners, not trespass, to use Flanagan's path by the leaf pile; Morgan, who has very bad manners, used it often.

Close trespass is another matter. Mehitabel sat on the roof of the sheep shed to make sure Morgan didn't come up the driveway into the space where Mehitabel is queen mother. For years she was the only female here except for her three cowed daughters, and while she ignored Barney's and Sidney's encroachments she stood guard against Morgan's. Gender is important to cats. Morgan sat across the drive on a woodpile, on her own side of an imaginary line drawn straight across from Mehitabel's fierce, beautiful owl eyes. Morgan understood; she and Mehitabel are birds of a feather in this lust for power and property.

Mehitabel's will stretched across the driveway like an electric eye, and I crossed it apprehensively as if it might be carcinogenic, though she wasn't hostile to me. Quite the contrary. She courted me lavishly, shamelessly; that would have been the final victory, to take me away from Morgan, to supplant her, move into her house and order her cast onto the dung heap for the crows. From the woodpile Morgan watched her, on the alert for any temporary failure of will or loss of nerve that would slacken the line and let her cross. Once, to see what would happen, I picked her up and carried her past Mehitabel; she struggled and scratched at me, leaped down, and dashed back to the woodpile. In the interplay of cat and cat, humans simply don't count. We can't, like the Greeks' gods, hang around the battlefield helping out our favorites; it's a breach of etiquette and our favorites wouldn't thank us and any victories we scored would be scrubbed from the record.

In a group as large as my sister's there is no pecking order. It would be mathematically impossible to keep track of, especially since these rankings have a way of shifting for no apparent reason. As in any group, though, there's always the last and least, usually the newcomer or junior member, but in this collection it's Snipe. All of us knew a kid like Snipe in school. If Snipe were a human eight-year-old he would come from the wrong side of the tracks, whine a lot, and smell of sour milk. He would wipe his nose on his coat sleeve all winter; the nurse would send home notes about things living in his hair. His ears would be full of scabby stuff, and when it came to choosing up teams the captains would come to blows over which had to take Snipe.

He's a narrow-chested, rat-faced, black and white cat with a hacking cough, made of poor protoplasm poorly put together, and no amount of nourishing food or veterinary attention has been able to improve on the hand nature dealt him. No matter who comes or goes in the household, Snipe is last, and knows it.

Among more primitive creatures like chickens or eight-year-olds, the others would simply fall on him and destroy him as a blot unworthy of existence, but Snipe goes unscathed. He is the opposite of threat. In a feline society where status is based on self-confidence, Snipe's well-founded humility is a *laissez-passer* and makes him invisible, crawling beneath everyone's notice like a low-flying plane avoiding radar. It's the cocky cat who may be asked to prove himself, though not if he's cocky enough.

For years Barney never had to prove a thing. His cockiness was so immense that no cat questioned it. Before he was neutered and set down among the common cats he lived like a sultan in his cattery; not for him the wearisome searches and the pleading serenade from the fence, the backyard skirmish and the torn ear. He never knew the meaning of failure or even competition, and year after year beautiful eager females were put into his cage without his even needing to ask. No other cat challenged his right to them. Success followed success. A life like that gets into the blood, literally. In groups of apes with a dominant male who gets all the best females, the subordinate male grows more and more subordinate, his confidence withers, and the testosterone in his blood sinks lower and lower. But take away the leader and he perks right up, his testosterone leaps, he beats his chest, chooses the prettiest mates, snatches everyone else's bananas, and becomes dominant himself. Barney, always the one and only, must have been pure testosterone by the time he retired.

He was castrated and disarmed into impotence, and it made no difference at all. In *The Fur Person*, castration reduces May Sarton's cat to humility overnight, but Barney's supercharged blood took years to cool down. Past the same line where Mehitabel's burning gaze kept Mor-

gan at bay, Barney sauntered unconcerned. He kept right
on going, through the garden bristling with astonished
cats on their own property, and up to the front door,
where he stared at the nearest human to open it. He
rarely uses his voice; he has rarely needed to. He walked
into the house and through the kitchen, and the resident
cats parted for him like the Red Sea. He never even
glanced at them. God knows what they thought; perhaps
they felt like the unfortunate Aztecs at the time of the
Spanish invasion: they had always had a legend that in-
vincible white gods were going to show up one of these
days, and by golly, here they were.

It was an appalling piece of effrontery, walking in like
that without asking, but he clearly didn't feel the need to
ask: does the sultan ask? His assumption of invulnera-
bility stunned the others into belief, and he came and
went when it pleased him, looking neither to left nor
right.

Very slowly the elixir drained from his blood. It seemed
to be a natural chemical process; there was no evidence that
any other cat ever challenged his godlike status. Vulnerabil-
ity crept up on him little by little. Within two years he
stopped going there unless I went with him, and then
he stopped going even with me. He began to defer occasionally to others, and sometimes even foolish Sidney
pushed him away from his dinner. The world was no longer
his; he stayed closer to home. When the kitten Morgan
bothered him, instead of grandly ignoring her or staring her
down, he stooped to hissing and sometimes backed away or
changed his path.

Deposed by his own chemistry, the sultan had become
just another one of the eunuchs. Still, he had had a grand
time while it lasted.

He has made no friends, though. Friendship in a cattery is
complicated by sex and the currents of protectiveness and
territoriality among so many unaltered cats and kittens, and
studs live in cages. For Barney, learning human friendship
came quickly and easily, but cat friendship never came; no

cat snuggles up to him, and he washes no cat's ears. He avoids interaction, and if he finds a cat in his favorite place, instead of asking permission to join it, or cuffing its head, or squeezing in on top of it, he simply walks away.

While challenge and strife may spring up among equals, in groups the hopelessly incompetent like Snipe are *hors de combat*, and the young or unfortunate are often tenderly protected. Derek Tangye describes a moving father-and-son relationship, with the father licking and cuddling his kitten and taking it for instructive walks. In *My Five Tigers* Lloyd Alexander documents the painstaking education of a new kitten by his two older, unrelated male cats. In *How to Live with a Cat* Margaret Cooper Gay mentions three abandoned starvelings she called the Joes, brought home to his own refrigerator by her cat Charlie. Another writer mentions a country tramp cat who was fed one day at a farmhouse and came back the next day with twenty-nine deserving friends. Colette's Long-Cat jumped into a cold and rushing stream to swim after, rescue, and drag back a drowning kitten, no relation of his. And then there was the Gray Cat.

The Gray Cat was an unaltered teenage male who came over regularly to play with my friend's small male kitten. This was in the city, and the Gray Cat, who plainly had a home, shouldn't have been allowed to travel around like that, but that's another story. The kitten's house was in a courtyard off the street, and he was let out to play there, with supervision from a window, and the Gray Cat played sweetly with him and taught him tag and wrestling.

There's a law in our city about dogs on leashes, but the only people who obey it are the owners of tiny fluffy dogs like animated dusters; people with Danes and Dobermans let them gallop on ahead, and stroll after them carrying the leash looped over the wrist with casual grace as if, like the riding crop, it existed mainly to decorate the owner. The gate of the courtyard was open and the Doberman, passing, saw the kitten outside alone. He sprang for it with the speed of a panther and the teeth of the great white shark. From nowhere the Gray Cat flashed into sight and leaped straight into his face. My friend, watching from a window, screamed simultaneously and rushed out waving her arms, but even so the dog had plenty of time to close his steel jaws just once and crush the Gray Cat to a pulp; that he didn't must have been due to his slow-wittedness in dealing with the unexpected. His owner arrived and, after inspecting his friend for scratches and delivering himself of a few words on the unwisdom of letting cats out into a dog's world, they departed.

Saved from the literal jaws of death, the kitten crept out from under a bush still fluffed, and the Gray Cat licked him on the head and shoulders before settling down to wash himself all over.

We can dismiss the heroism of a mother cat as mainly instinct, a blind urging in her nerves and muscles that she has no choice but to obey, but what can we say about the Gray Cat? If it had been a human that he saved, a deed of a quite different and far higher order, of course, no doubt he would have been invited to the White House and given a medal and it would have been on the evening news, but the kitten was only a kitten, and so the Gray Cat was allowed to go about his business.

If in a colony cats seem largely to ignore one another, among individuals and in smaller families they often go beyond tolerance to develop genuine personal affections for each other. All proper behaviorists base cat relationships firmly on dominance and submission, but the closet inspection of my family of five shows no evidence of it at all. Even in his sultan days Barney imposed his will on no other cat, and took no other cat's space or food. No cat here is in charge, no cat here submits; they all have their personal crotchets, but no one seems to care who's first. Maybe the behaviorists have studied too many families of a mother with grown children. Mothers tend to maintain their sway. Or maybe my cats are simply lazy; with more than one or two other cats around, upholding a superior position is a lot of work, which cats avoid, and involves contention, which unsexed cats avoid as destructive of peace and naptime.

My group seems to have melded itself into a family of such wordless solidarity, and to take such evident comfort from each other, that I sometimes suppress a twinge of envy. There are chronic washers and washees among them, but this is personality, not dominance; Sidney never did learn to wash himself. Barney sits apart from the others, but he's one of them, a member if not a friend. When the little black cat was sick and got well again and came back from the vet with her bandages finally off there was a spontaneous rejoicing of great giddiness all around the house and up and down the stairs, more like a dance than a game, and even Barney joined in.

They parcel me out among themselves in my different times and places. At the typewriter I am Morgan's, to climb on my shoulder and bite my face and stand on the repeating keys. Reading the Sunday paper I am Barney's and sometimes the little black cat's; she's new and still pushing herself into place. Barney also waits on my bed at night to claim those first few minutes before Corvo takes over. In my sleep I am Morgan's from the collarbone up, Corvo's from collarbone to waist, and Barney's from the waist down, while the black cat free-lances. My daughter is Sidney's, and no one questions his possession. Behind this sharing there's no grand abstract notion of fairness, only a reasonable cooperation to minimize stress.

There's a basket here that sits on the table under a lamp, and it's the premier cat place in the house. There's room in it for only one of the big cats, though the two smaller ones can squeeze in and share. The basket would belong to the dominant cat if we had a dominant cat, but its occupants rotate regularly and peacefully; the cat in possession is never challenged or chivvied, and when it leaves possession passes to the first cat to notice the vacancy. Perhaps I've just made an accidental lucky selection of feline equals, or perhaps cat society isn't as ambitiously human as it's been painted. Perhaps scientific laboratory conditions are the wrong place to inspect the cat.

Cats who are friends will lick each other, with special attention to the head and ears, wrestle, stalk each other from behind the furniture, and conduct noisy games of tag up and down the stairs and through the bric-a-brac. They will play a noncompetitive form of hockey or billiards with a ball or a walnut, with a lot of strategic cat-positioning behind chair legs and a hunkering of haunches for the spring. It takes two cats to play the bag game properly. You drop an empty grocery bag on the floor so the top is open, and one cat gets into it, rustling interestingly. The second cat pounces on the bag, the first cat springs out from ambush, and both pretend to be surprised. Then the second cat gets in the bag. Repeat steps two through four. There are no winners. There are rarely winners in a cat game. When it gets too rough or one cat gets bored, the game stops by mutual consent; it's enough to stop any game just to sit down and wash.

The sterner authorities insist that cats don't actually *play*, that only humans have the concept of play and all the games of cats are merely to keep themselves in training for hunting mice, but this view is narrowly based on human experience, in which all games are merely to keep ourselves in training for business competition or war. Maybe only cats have the concept of play.

The *Britannica* warns us that having two young cats of the same age may make training and discipline difficult. It doesn't say what it was trying to accomplish in the way of training, or what happened, but I have a vision of, instead of one obediently intimidated kitten, two of them, adolescent confederates, crouched giggling together in a corner while the *Britannica* stamped its foot and bellowed commands in a rage of impotence and fired warning shots into the ceiling. Perhaps the *Britannica* isn't temperamentally cat people. And if we have no cat and want two cats, two from the same litter will already be friends and need no introduction.

There are authoritative instructions for introducing a new cat to an established cat or cats. You can set up a screen door of baby-gate between rooms to separate them while they get acquainted. You can keep them closed up in separate rooms, and then switch rooms, giving them a chance to get used to each other through the residual scent markers, but I'm not sure about this; it wouldn't work with me. I'd feel much worse knowing an invisible stranger was lurking around the premises, like lying in bed listening to assassins downstairs that turn out to be only an errant brother blundering around in the dark.

I've always just dumped the cats on each other, with varying results. Probably no matter how it's done there'll be a certain amount of hissing, but I've never had a conflict that lasted more than a couple of days. Maybe some of it's in our minds. Our civilized tradition of hospitality is outraged, and our feelings ache vicariously for the one received so brutally in its new home, like an orphan out of Dickens. The cats don't feel that way, though. It's normal to them, this defense of home and privilege against strangers, and then the gradual acceptance of stranger as resident, and the new one has never read Dickens. It knows full well it's intruding, that its entry-level position is on the bottom, or even in a closet or under the bed, and its job is to cringe and ingratiate, proceed slowly, and look for room for advancement later, seizing small opportunities to encroach.

When there might be real bloodshed, we can put it away somewhere, let things simmer down, try again, keep an eye on developments.

The more cats, the easier; for a longtime only cat a new one is a darker threat than if there have always been plural cats, as a new baby is more upsetting to an only child than to a houseful of children. And young cats are easier. Cats, sometimes grudgingly, are careful of the young, and probably the resident cat will eventually, with some grumblings and backsliding, admit the kitten's claim on care and lick its head. Especially if we ourselves aren't taking terribly good care of it. A kitten sobbing in a corner for its mother is a lot more appealing to our cat than a kitten purring on our lap. This seems hard on the kitten, but it doesn't have our sentimental overview, our dual mind in which we both suffer and redouble our sufferings by watching ourselves suffer, and comparing our condition to the happiness of nonsufferers. It will feel better soon. Pat the old cat, let the new one cry awhile.

Not all cats take to group living. Cats vary. Cats vary so widely that all data is meaningless and the professional classifiers gnash their teeth trying to come up with even a single fact common to all.

Some cats, for whatever reason, are as solitary as their reputation would have them; some strike up close, enduring friendships with other cats and mourn bitterly when they leave or die; some have no use for cats and care only for their humans. There is even unnerving evidence that some nonfamilial cats gather in groups for social purposes.

This goes against everything we think we know. Aside from impromptu gatherings around females in heat, which are marred by loud noises and occasional warfare, a cat should not be a joiner, should disdain bylaws and secret handshakes and cocktail parties. His independence from social entanglements is part of what we like about him. Dogs, yes; dogs hang out together in groups on street corners, socializing and sniffing each other's rear ends, but they're pack animals; it's their tradition to do so. Cats, no.

Just the same, the literature of superstition is full of secret cat meetings. The cats in these tales are usually witches or demons in disguise, or accompanied by actual witches and/or devils, and nobody is up to any good. In the ancient story "The King of the Cats," the traveler comes across a funeral procession of cats, en route to bury their leader. Since the cat is known to be a solitary, where did these tales come from; what terrified peasant came upon a group of them, and did the unlikeliness of it make it all the more sinister?

Lloyd Alexander claims that his cat Rabbit joined a local club and attended its meetings in an outbuilding in a nearby field; there were perhaps a dozen members, he says, and meetings lasted until two or three in the morning, with occasional all-nighters. Later his young Siamese David formed a group of his own that met in the basement, coming in through a broken window, and these seemed to be the younger cats of the neighborhood. They were neither fighting nor making love, the two accepted social activities of cats. They were just *there*, apparently taking some unfeline pleasure in the company.

I would have assumed that all the members were male, like Shriners, but animal psychologist Dr. Michael W. Fox thinks not. In his splendid book *Understanding Your Cat* he says, "Gatherings of cats, which have nothing to do with mating, often occur at night. They are purely social ... Male and female cats will congregate at a meeting place not far from their home range when they sit quite close, even engaging in mutual grooming and licking. Occasional hostility may be seen, such as hissing and ear flattening, but these gatherings are generally peaceful and, interestingly, occur *outside* the mating season. Around midnight the meeting may quietly disperse and each cat will return to its sleeping quarters."

And these are the same creatures that go to such lengths to avoid even crossing each other's paths in the woods?

Boy had no interest in other cats and gave his undivided attention to me. As other household cats came and went he walked among them apparently barely distinguishing one from another, and washed his own ears.

Then we rented a house in a seaside town for a month in the summer, and took Boy with us. I let him out, and he sniffed the premises and presently came back. Within a few days, however, something had happened. He had to go out, urgently, every evening at nine o'clock, and he returned promptly at five in the morning, somehow scaling the side of the house and scratching at the screen of the window over my bed. He slept most of the day, and in the late afternoon began prowling the windowsills, looking out. It rained a lot that month, and whatever it was was canceled if it rained. If it was still raining at six or seven he seemed quite frantic, checking the sky from every window as if he had planned a picnic for forty people that might have to be moved into the living room. If it was still raining at nine he gave up and slept that night on my feet, where he had always slept before. Otherwise he hardly noticed me.

I was hurt. This was my major cat, my close friend, and he had never before followed any routine but mine, going to bed when I did and getting up with me in the morning, and now something in this temporary town was more important to him than I was.

I have no evidence that a group of cats, probably many of them vacationing transients and strangers to each other, met every night in Stone Harbor, New Jersey; that Boy, a lifelong loner, was invited to join, and did; that they met by prearrangement at a certain hour and broke up just before five in the morning; but I haven't got any other explanations, either. On previous vacations in the country he'd gone out only casually, and slept in my bed at night. He was not equipped for making love, and there was no evidence that he went hunting; he never hunted. Sometimes a cat will take on a second home, and two families, unknown to each other, will feed him and consider him their own, but why visit so late at night when most humans are sleeping, and who would let him out again before dawn? Besides, he was my cat as no other cat has ever been, and I can't suspect him of disloyalty with other humans. But something out there took him away from me every night unless it rained.

And it was important to him. Instead of strolling out the door, pausing to consider the prospect and inspect objects of interest, he hurried away like a man with an appointment, and always in the same direction. He was black all over, and he would have been in deep trouble in the fifteenth and sixteenth centuries; it would have been my duty, anyone's duty, to kill him instantly if he'd hastened away like that on St. John's Eve, or the second Wednesday in

Lent, or All Hallows' Eve, or most of the nights in between.

At the end of the month we went back to the city and took up our normal lives, and he slept in bed and never even glanced out of a window. Still, there had been that month, and I thought about it. I assume that, if there ever really were demonic cats out covening, by now and in a sleepy little American beach town they must have degenerated from their unholy purposes to the sort of beery conviviality associated with Elks and Moose, but I'll never know. However long you have a cat and however plainly he lays his life open before you, there is always something hidden, some name he goes by in a place you never heard of.

The French psychologist Leyhausen compares cat relationships to those of a paranoically unsociable human, and Fernand Méry, agreeing, adds that even the friendship of siblings ends the moment they're able to hunt and fend for themselves. But environment does affect sociability, and when the struggle to survive eases off, surely a cat, most adaptable of creatures, can lay down the sword and indulge in the luxury of a friend, even a club full of friends?

There are also reports of ownerless cats living free in communities with a kind of social structure, or government.

Most of the stories come from Italy, especially Rome. Cats there, they say, live in a colony or federation of colonies and submit to a sort of law or code of behavior. If a cat commits a heinous crime—and no one has been able to report on what constitutes a crime among cats; kitten murder, perhaps—that cat is expelled from the colony. Ostracized; shunned, as among the Amish. And it is further said that a cat so shunned falls into despair and may commit suicide by running under a moving car. Given the nature of traffic in Rome, it seems a bit thick to attribute intention to a run-over cat, but that's the story.

In *Rome and a Villa* Eleanor Clark reports that the Roman cats seem not to be wandering freely around the city but keep together in a clearly defined asylum area. In a market square, Piazza Vittorio, she watched a group of

about 150 going about their business and sunning themselves on the remains of a great ruined fountain, completely
relaxed and at home, washing each other's heads. They
were well-mannered and there was no fighting, no scars or
chewed ears. When a sudden rainstorm struck they all
dashed for shelter, but not for the closest shelter; apparently
each had a prearranged niche under an eave or in a cranny
and made for it in an orderly fashion, with no confusion or
squabbling. They weren't thin, being fed on a kind of semi-
official basis, and they enjoyed a life midway between
childish dependency and the perils of utter wilderness.

Maybe we're being presumptuous in assuming that there
is even such a thing as cat "behavior." Opportunistic, flexible, perhaps almost reasonable, maybe a cat can behave in
any way at all that seems consonant with its own best interests. Unlike the confused, neurotic human, bewildered by
guilt and aspirations, a cat can usually assess its choices
and act accordingly.

They have few prejudices. A cat that lives with different
creatures learns to explain itself to them, if not with subtlety, then at least well enough to build a relationship, and
affectionate friendships have sprung up between cats and
horses, roosters, goats, rabbits, guinea pigs, wild foxes,
and even canaries. More than half the households with cats
have dogs as well, and everyone usually gets along. Sometimes it's only a guarded neutrality, but often they're deeply
attached, and a well-disposed dog will defend its cat from
other dogs. One cat in the literature required her dog to
move her kittens for her from place to place in the house.
She was a restless mother, constantly looking for better
nests for her babies, and when she found one she went to
the dog, and he followed her to the kittens and picked up
each one very gently by the scruff of the neck and followed
her with it to the new site.

People worry that a cat raised among dogs will be too
trusting of strange dogs, but even the dimmest cat distinguishes between family members and outsiders, and all cats
consider the circumstances. A cat in a safe place may tease

a dog unmercifully; a cat that knows a dog is chained knows the precise circumference of the chain; turn the dog loose and the cat retires discreetly up a tree.

A cat of ours was regularly chased by a neighborhood dog, who dropped by almost daily for the purpose, until she had kittens. The next day the dog trotted into the yard as usual, and she sprang at him and scrambled onto his head and clawed his eyes and nose and rode him howling up the street. She had been chased by consent only, and now the game was over. Forever after when the dog had to pass our house he left the sidewalk and detoured widely into the safety of the street.

In an area with nothing to climb and loose dogs prowling in pairs or teams, we might worry. But indoors, within the family, as often as not it's the dog who gets bullied. Poor scruffy Vicky was intimidated by cats all her life until the kitten Gregory came. She'd always admired cats, and here finally was one that didn't scorn her company. A childless dog, she took him for her own, and held him between her paws and washed and washed him, crooning, until he was sopping wet. When he'd had enough he escaped to barricade himself behind a row of cookbooks for a nap, while Vicky sat in front of the shelf and mooed lonesomely for him. Alas, when he got older he realized it was an undignified relationship for a cat, and scorned her like the others.

Cats and dogs rarely fight like cats and dogs. Beyond a temperamental difference, there's no real reason for war; cats and dogs aren't items in each other's diets, and they aren't rivals in the hunting field like cats and owls. (Cats can be an item of owl diet, which is why a wise cat checks the sky before leaving the house, and why a nervous cat likes to be under something, and why the approach to a strange cat is from its eye level instead of from high.)

It's natural for a dog to chase small animals that run away, but the dog may not be thinking "cat," as distinct from "rabbit" or "squirrel." Since nothing else chases a cat on foot, the cat may be thinking "dog," and Morgan is categorically afraid of them, though that might be maternal teaching. The others stand their ground: if they run the dog will run after them. It's traditional.

In the town of Chanhu-daro in India, a dog chased a cat across some fresh-made bricks before they dried, and their paw prints are still there, the pursuing dog's pressed in over the fleeing cat's. They've been there for four thousand years.

6

The Cat's Early Years

Nobody seems to know for certain what a cat is or where is came from, though everyone has a theory.

Pliny tells us that, some six hundred years before the Prophet, Arabs worshiped a golden cat and believed that there was such special cleanliness and purity about cats that their origin must have been distinct from that of ordinary creatures. One Arab version has it that one of the lions on the Ark sneezed and brought forth the cat to control the shipboard mice; another, less ethereal, holds that the male monkey got bored with his watery confinement and took to playing around with the lionness, their relationship producing the first two cats.

In classical mythology Apollo created the lion to scare his sister Diana, and to tease him she mocked his invention by creating the cat.

In the West of Ireland they say that at some turning point in the world's history the snakes turned into cats, which is why the cat's bite is venomous.

More prosaically, in the beginning was Miacis, a weasel-like creature of the Eocene age some 40 or 50 million years ago, who branched out into various specialties; some of them were small cats. Cats developed early in mammalian history and guessed right the first time; they looked like cats back when most mammals' ancestors were still unrecognizably experimental. Between 7 and 40 million years ago, depending on which book you read, a cat was already a cat.

That much seems widely believed. But when we narrow it down to the present-day house cat, all is confusion.

The first famous cats were Egyptian, which proves only that imperial gods leave records that endure for five thousand years, and house pets don't.

Was the Egyptian cat the same as our cat? Were there *two* Egyptian cats? Some scholars insist that there are two types in the paintings and carvings, one with short ears and a blunt nose, one fox-faced with a sharp nose and pointy ears. All were short-haired and ginger-colored or tawny, with black markings.

In 1907, an expedition into Egypt sent back to the British Museum a box of 192 cat skulls from the cat burying grounds at Gizeh, dating from around 600 to 200 B.C. Some years later, when he got around to opening the box, Dr. T.C.S. Morrison-Scot said the skulls were of two types, one resembling *Felis chaus* and one *Felis libyca*, both small wild cats still around in North Africa today. *Libyca* is long-faced and big-eared, with ticked fur like our modern Abyssinians. It has white toes and is familiarly known as the Gloved Cat; tribes in the eastern Sudan still tame it from the wild. *Libyca* is a desert cat, *chaus* a jungle cat, more Asian than African, sandy brown with black tufts on its ear tips and very shy. Somehow, so late in the day of the Egyptian cat cult, they were still distinct enough for Dr. Morrison-Scot to tell apart, and hadn't blurred together over a thousand years of close association. There were fewer of the *chaus* type. Most of the skulls he examined were of the *libyca* type but somewhat bigger than normal, and bigger than our house cats' skulls but smaller than *chaus*'s. He thought these might be a separate strain, and tried calling it *Felis libyca bubastis*, but the idea never caught on.

The *Encyclopedia Americana* throws us an alternative to *chaus, Felis ocreata*, another African. (Unless, of course, they're two different names for the same cat. The naming of cats, as T. S. Eliot points out, is a difficult matter.)

Some authorities say cats weren't originally from Egypt at all, but were brought in from Ethiopia; several state firmly that they were brought by Sesotris after his conquest of Nubia. Méry suggest that they have no true wild ancestors, that the Egyptians discovered a mutation, something different that interested them enough to cosset and breed it, effectively inventing their own cats.

At different points in history we start to run across the sturdy, round-faced cat of Europe, a slender, long-faced cat in Thailand, and chubby, fuzzy cats and tailless cats in Japanese and Chinese paintings. And what of the blue-eyed jungle cats of Southeast Asia, and the chunky, long-haired Persian and the slim long-haired Angora, and the Siamese with its knobbed tail, raucous voice, and different estrous cycle? How may cats are there? Science would prefer to name a single cat, a single point of origin, a single ancestor; it would be unprofessionally messy to have various cats developing here and there from various genetic material.

To compound the problem, British authorities feel that, since Britain is the only part of the world that really matters, no merely North African cat can be a real cat, a proper cat, and therefore *Felis* as we know her must be descended in part from *Felis sylvestris*, the European wildcat and a British subject that some say is still common and widespread and others say is almost extinct. Linnaeus thought he had disproved this conclusively in 1736, but many scholarly modern sources still state the connection as a recognized fact—Egyptian cat + *sylvestris* = proper cat— and add that our house cats still breed freely with wildcats. Other authorities, equally positive, say this rarely happens, and when it does the kittens are sickly and sterile. Some claim *sylvestris* has a very different bone structure from puss, and can't be related.

We could almost conjecture that some of these science people aren't making a clear distinction between *sylvestris* proper and puss herself in the woods, homeless for generations and hissing and scratching when grabbed up by marauding scientists, but still genetically one of our own.

It seems safest to go with Linnaeus on the wildcat matter. In its pictures *sylvestris* looks quite dauntingly savage and morose. It's said to be untamable even when taken in infancy, and it grows up to be a burly and powerful opponent; in Scotland's surviving tales of man versus wildcat, the wildcat often wins. This doesn't seem like a promising basis for a friendship. Surely an amiable inclination to get along with mankind brought puss to our hearths in the first place, and the self-confident Gloved Cat and shy *chaus* seem more likely to have bequeathed it.

Alas for eurochauvinism, the evidence of origin seems weighted in favor of North Africa, though Darwin said Asia, and another source says *libyca* is as much Asian as African. And domestic cats were mentioned in Chinese and Sanskrit writings from several thousand years ago, though they may not be quite the same cats we're talking about. There's a modern domestic cat in India, small and spotted, that looks a lot like *Felis ornata*, a desert cat that still runs wild there and interbreeds with house cats.

Cats of one kind or another, large and small, are native to all continents except Australia and Antarctica; many of them, though visibly different, are cross-fertile. I don't see why we need to narrow it down to a single, historically verified, proto-house cat, especially since no one seems able to. Many small cats can be tamed. No one knows why.

The business of tamability doesn't much interest historians; no one wonders what it means, this inclination to our society, or why it should happen at all. It's quite reasonable that so many wild creatures can't be tamed even when caught young and gently treated; it seems vastly strange that some are naturally pleased to share their lives with us even under circumstances, as must have happened often, when their own world was just as comfortable as ours, or more so. Scholars who believe that humans have only to will a thing in order to accomplish it say we "tamed" cats because they caught rats and mice, but who among us has an owl or a blacksnake asleep on our couch? There must have been some give-and-take, a willingness on the cat's part, or we would have had a prisoner instead of a friend. Northerners like Kipling make much of fire and warmth as a lure, but the first tame cats of record lived in mild and pleasant climates.

Cats are the only domestic animals that came to us from independent lives of their own. All of the rest of our retinue arrived with innate traditions of pack or flock or herd, of follow-the-leader, of submission to a superior or to the common law of the group. Only the cat had always made its own decisions. It decided in our favor, for reasons we will never know.

All we know for certain of the early days is that some millions of years ago cat-type animals appeared, and then some five or six thousand years ago the Egyptians were tripping over a cat in the kitchen, and calling it "mau."

Why did they call it "mau"? You'll never guess. *Mau* is also the Egyptian word for seeing or for light, and because of the reflecting layer of tapetum behind a cat's eyes that makes them glow in the dark, and the way the pupils contract and expand, cats came to be associated with light, and more specifically with the changeable moon that hoards the sun's light for us during the dark hours; hence "mau."

This is an example of scientific reconstruction at its finest. Not for scientists the offhand supposition that they might have called it something *before* they decided its eyes were like the moon; not for them the humble domestic scenario:

"There's something at the door that says 'mau,' and it wants to come in."

"Is it dangerous?"

"No, it's quite small. Sometimes it makes a humming sound, then it rubs against my legs and says 'mau.' "

"Let it come in, then."

"Come in, Mau."

No cat ever came to the door and said "cat." It's a most unfeline syllable, and its origins are another flurry of confusion. It shows up in Latin and Greek around the first century A.D., although one source tells us Herodotus was using *kattos* four hundred years earlier, and said it was an Egyptian word. An ancient writer says the Latin *catus* is from *cattare*, which in turn is from *captare oculis*, "to catch by seeing." In 1658 *The Historie of Four-Footed Beastes* said it came from the Latin *cautus*, meaning "cautious." Untouched by Latin, the Zoroastrians called it *gatu*. One scholar says the Latin comes from "African languages" by way of Arabic, Syrian, and Greek. The *Oxford English Dictionary* offers us "catt," "catte," "kat," and "katte," but says it's of unknown origin.

"Puss," on the other hand, comes from Bastet, or Bast, or Pasht, the Egyptian cat-headed goddess. The pleasant thing about feline scholarship is that anyone can play; your guess is as good as theirs, and I'd like to submit "puss" as coming from "Pss!", the sound you make when you'd like a cat to stop ripping the furniture. Because it approximates the hiss of a hostile cat, your cat will probably glance up at you, if not actually desist from ripping, as even the Egyptians may have noticed. I admit it doesn't sound very scholarly, but I submit it anyway. It's better than "to catch by seeing."

Even the scientific classifications are subject to argument. The *OED* calls puss *Felis domesticus* and the wildcat *Felis catus*, but the *Britannica* admits of no *domesticus* and uses *catus* for house cats and house cats only. Some authorities call the wildcat *sylvestris*; others consider it the same as a house cat and call it whatever they're calling her. The American bobcat is sometimes set apart as *Felis rufa* and sometimes lumped together with *Felis lynx*. The problem seems to be that classifications are based on skulls and teeth, an area where all cat-creatures are so similar that science has trouble telling one from another, except for the cheetah, which has nonretractable claws, and likes to go for walks on a leash and is arguably more dog than cat.

In paintings and statues the Egyptians' cat, whoever she

was, sits tall and narrow and stately with her back very straight, as befits divinity.

In the early days there was nothing cuddly about the Egyptian cat gods. The Book of the Dead is said by some to have been already ancient at the time of the First Dynasty in 5650 B.C., though others move it up to 3500; a papyrus copy of it from 1580 B.C. offers us an early glimpse of the Great Cat Ra, the male cat, the sun-god cat. Sir Ernest Budge's translation begins, "I am the Cat which fought near the Persea Tree in Heliopolis on the night when the foes of Neb-er-tcher were destroyed." The illustration shows a ferocious-looking cat slicing into a huge snake with a knife; the snake is Set, the serpent of evil and darkness. Eclipses of the sun in Egypt became re-enactments of this primal battle between the snake-forces of darkness and the cat-forces of light; everyone turned out into the streets to cheer for the cat. The cat kept the world safe from darkness. The cat slept curled in a circle like the moon, clearly showing that it was also in charge of tides, weather, and crops. With connections like that the cat was to go far.

At Thebes, on the royal tombs of the Nineteenth and Twentieth Dynasties, an inscription reads, "Praise be to thee, O Ra, exalted Sekhem, thou art the Great Cat, the avenger of the gods, and the judge of words, and the president of the sovereign chiefs, and the governor of the holy Circle, thou art indeed the bodies of the Great Cat."

The female cat represented a mother-goddess called Mut, later Bastet, Bast, Pasht, Ubastet, or Bubastis; the Egyptians were easygoing about names. Some say Bastet was the offspring of the sun god Osiris (or Ra or Horus or Ptah) and his wife Isis, while others hold that Isis was a later evolution of Bastet. Somehow Hathor, goddess of pleasure, was involved in it too. Maybe the Egyptians could keep all this straight in their heads, or maybe they didn't bother and just let the priests worry about it.

The earliest portrait of the cat-headed Bastet is in a Fifth Dynasty temple dating from around 3000 B.C. Mut/Bastet was in charge of motherhood, and sex, and fertility, but in another aspect she was connected with Sekhnet, the lion-headed goddess of war, death, and sickness. She also supervised good health, and music and dancing, and crops, and hunting, and wisdom, and happiness.

Some scholars suggest that, though sacred, the cat wasn't necessarily domesticated much before 1500 B.C. But there's a picture from 2600 B.C. of a cat wearing a collar, and it isn't easy to put a collar on a cat you're not personally acquainted with.

Certainly from 1500 B.C. paintings and carvings show the erstwhile ferocious warrior cat Ra and the great mother Bast now very much at home in Egyptian family and social life and living well, jeweled and pampered. That was the year a temple was dedicated to Bastet at Beni-Hassan on the Nile, and from all over Egypt people sent their cats to be buried there, embalmed, spiced, and mummified, with turquoise collars around their necks and cloth ears and painted eyes. In the nineteenth century, excavation of this site yielded three hundred thousand cat mummies, along with some mummified mice as food for the long journey. They were shipped to England and auctioned off as fertilizer, the auctioneer, according to a newspaper report, using a stiffly mummified cat as a gavel. They brought around eighteen dollars a ton. Considering the extensive Egyptian curses invoked by even the accidental molesting of even a single cat, it would be interesting to learn what happened afterwards to the fertilizer entrepreneurs and the auctioneer, and their descendents.

Sacred as they were, Egyptian domestic cats were no mere decorations. They were companions. In 1400 B.C., we see a cat retrieving a duck for a hunter, and in another picture a man whose name is given as Mutsa has taken his family and his cat fishing and duck hunting; the cat is eagerly poised to leap in and bring back the duck. There seems to have been a doglike tone to the relationship: the cat gets taken along. In a New Kingdom (1570–1075 B.C.) carving, Queen Tiyi is in a canoe with her daughters, sitting on a chair, and a brisk-looking striped cat sits under the chair and enjoys the outing. Any modern apartment cat would envy it.

The cat came to banquets. In one scene, the woman has tied her cat to the leg of her chair, where it's trying to unfasten itself to get to a bowl of food just out of reach. In another, a cat with a ring in its ear sits under the woman's chair while the man holds a kitten on his lap; the kitten plays with his sleeve. At another banquet, the cat under the chair is eating a fish. Under a chair has always been a good place for cats; it keeps them from getting tripped over and offers access to dropped fish.

In the temples the high priests watched the temple cats day and night for the omens and prophecies spelled out by how they slept and woke and stretched, and held their tails and whiskers. The expression in their eyes told whether or not the sick would recover. In the street, a man who found a dead cat had to run away screaming and lamenting, lest someone think he had killed it himself, even by accident; killing a cat was punishable by death from stoning. In the house, if the family cat died the family shaved off their eyebrows and went into deep mourning, and the body was mummified at all possible expense. If the house caught fire, the cat had to be rescued first. At adolescence, children had a cat's silhouette tattooed on their arms to call down the blessings of Bastet on their lives. At human funerals, the deceased held an ivory wand with a cat's head to guard him on his trip to the land of the dead; various later traditions in other countries took up the cat as guide and protector of the soul after death.

The Egyptians seem to have had no trouble connecting the powerful supernatural goddess with the cat curled up at the foot of the bed or begging scraps in the kitchen; they were the same, and not the same, a difficult concept for us whose deities have been centralized and invisible for so long. Religion was tangible and flexible, and divinity flickered like an antic lightning from host to host. Priests wove their own colors into the rationale. First causes, if there were any, were not only lost, they were unimportant. Perhaps in the beginning cats had something to do with lions; the dangerous cats have always been nervously respected, and jaguars were worshiped as gods in pre-Columbian Mexico, Guatemala, and Peru. A cat could have originally represented a lion, been a sort of ambassador from lionhood to be propitiated, and its cultivation a symbolic truce with lions, or a kinship with their powers. (I hasten to add that this is just me talking to myself, and the notion has no basis in any sort of scholarship whatever, but the historians' insistence on the practical benefits of cats seems almost too simple to be true. Mouse hunting is reason enough to keep cats but not to worship them.)

Bubastis, center of cat worship, became the capital of all Egypt, and in April and May some seven hundred thousand pilgrims gathered there for the yearly festival of Bastet. By most accounts it was the kind of party that in modern times would have ended with tear gas and fire hoses. The annual religious duty of the faithful around 950 B.C. was to spend the spring drinking heavily and making public love to one and all to set an example for the season's crops. Those who were unable to make the pilgrimage heard the roistering boats go by on the Nile and began their own sacred duties in the streets of their hometowns.

It all sounds a bit rowdy for a cat's taste, and probably the objects of this devotion were glad to take up their customary positions under chairs while the party raged.

In 500 B.C., the Persian king Cambyses invaded Egypt and laid successful siege to the city of Pelusium, giving birth to a tale that turns up in various versions from various scholarly sources, each solemnly represented as historical fact. In one version, the Persians threw live cats over the walls of the city, which blasphemy so panicked the Egyptian defenders that they ran distracted till the city fell. A second version says the Persians carried cats instead of shields, and naturally no Egyptian could touch them for fear of harming a cat and incurring the death penalty himself. Version three says simply that the Egyptians refused to engage in battle at all lest a cat in the city be accidentally hurt, and so surrendered without a blow exchanged. The fourth version says that Cambyses ordered his soldiers to search the area and collect all the cats, and then attacked the town driving a horde of cats before him, each soldier carrying a live cat, and the Egyptians surrendered to protect them.

Somehow the whole episode seems odd. Even in those far-off times cats had claws, and a natural aversion to being thrown over walls or snatched up and clutched as shields by strange soldiery. And as for rounding up hundreds of cats for this base purpose in an area where they were held sacred, how did the Persians manage that? Were they starving strays; were gods allowed to wander loose and starving? And even if they were, consider the problem of the average Persian foot soldier chasing a stray cat across fields and down alleys with which the cat was more familiar than the man. And what of the populace, the Egyptians outside the besieged city; what were they doing while an army chased their cats? Did the soldiers burst into their houses and kidnap their personal cats, when a cat is so small and easy to hide and an Egyptian would fight like a tiger to defend it? And how do you drive a horde of cats before you? Cats are not sheep. The vision of a Persian army organizing a mass of angry, terrified cats and moving them in a forward direction toward a designated goal is hard to entertain no matter how deep one's respect for historians.

It all sounds a little like a contemporary joke, translated and solemnized in later centuries, as if one of our political cartoons were unearthed and reported as gospel: see, their president held hands with a bomb, or see, a donkey sat in their Senate. Maybe after the fall of Pelusium some local wag made it up to tease the defeated commander, or maybe he made it up himself as an excuse, and the versions developed by word of mouth for a while before anyone wrote them down. I for one don't believe anything except that Pelusium fell to Cambyses, while the local cats went padding about their apolitical purposes underfoot.

Still, Egypt's strong feelings about cats were clearly beginning to affect international matters. There were cat troubles with Greece. Egypt had passed laws making it illegal to sell cats out of the country, so the Greeks, bothered by rats and mice and weary of dealing with the voracious and disagreeable weasels they used to catch them, stole cats. They supported a regular pirate trade in cats, with severe diplomatic repercussions. Egypt even sent missions around the Mediterranean ports trying to buy back her cats, with only moderate success. A Greek bas-relief from the fifth century A.D. shows a cat on a leash about to attack a dog, so clearly some very tough specimens were leaking out to the larger world. (An entirely different line of thought holds that the Greeks had no domestic cats, valuing them only for their fur, which was widely worn by the poor, and the cat was on a leash to keep it from escaping an arranged fight with the dog.)

In the first century B.C., during a delicate period in Egypt's relations with Rome, a Roman soldier killed a cat by accident and was mobbed by the Egyptian crowds in spite of frantic official attempts at intervention. According to one report, he was killed and his body dragged through the streets, and the incident led to a series of reprisals and rebellions that plagued international relations all the way to the suicide of Cleopatra and Egypt's decline.

Cats continued to spread. The Phoenician sailors, mobile traders of the eastern Mediterranean since the tenth century B.C., probably carried them, deliberately or accidentally or both; sailors have always had a soft spot for cats, and Phoenicians always had a sharp eye for trade goods. Some say they carried them as far as England. Some say cats found their way through Europe by way of Greece, and others that the Roman legions took them, part of the "impedimenta" Caesar was always complaining about; cat remains have been found in Roman villas in Britain.

In Rome, where today officially protected cats sleep in the sun on Keats's and Shelley's graves, the cat became a tutelary spirit, no longer a reigning deity in charge of all the major aspects of life and death, but a humble hearth watcher. With the mental split we still manage today, the Romans considered her both a protector of the home and an emblem of liberty. They were a cleanly people for their time, and no doubt admired the immaculate cat, but probably their straight-edged military minds were never deeply tuned to the feline.

It's said that the Greek general Galsthelos, who commanded Pharaoh's army, fled to Portugal after his defeat when the Red Sea parted. He took along his wife Scota, the Pharaoh's beautiful daughter, who naturally brought her cats. Centuries later their descendant, Fergus I, became ruler of a northern kingdom he called Scotland after his ancestress, and introduced to Britain the descendants of her cats.

Accepted opinion puts cats in Gaul in the fourth or fifth century A.D., by which time they were catching mice as far away as China, but there's a statuette and a table pedestal from the first or second century that shows them already comfortably established there. The statuette wears a collar and looks entirely domestic; the cat on the pedestal is held by a small boy and wears a bell to frighten off evil spirits. All the early Gallic cats look cuddlier than the Egyptian, rounder and fatter, and are shown being clutched and carried in awkward positions, often by children, gods no more.

The pragmatic historians keep reminding us that the cat spread around the world following the spread of rats and mice, and was taken up by humans solely to protect granaries—or, in China, silkworm cocoons—from rodent teeth. They tell us that back when man was a hunter the cat was hated as a rival in the hunting field (though I've found no early paintings of men hunting mice for the table), and that as farming and grain storing spread, the cat became accepted as an ally.

No one will admit of cats as self-indulgence.

Maybe history exaggerates the utilitarian. Maybe we're attributing too much common sense to our ancestors. We assume that, since their lives were harsher than ours, or seem so from our complacent viewpoint, they had no time for sentiment, and no one would invite a pretty cat indoors on a cold night or carry home a cheerful two-months kitten without an eye to usefulness.

Of course, we like to believe we're nicer now than people used to be, more sensitive, imaginative, generous. And it's true we've been through, or cats have been through, periods of hideous cruelty in the embarrassingly recent past. It's comforting to tell ourselves we're getting better all the time, in a straight line through history, and if people three hundred years ago tortured cats without regard for their pain, then people a thousand years ago must have been inconceivably crueler. Unless favored by superstition, as in Egypt, cats must have been suffered to live at all only under mouse-catching covenants.

And again, we look backward through the glass of Victorian scholarship, when everyone believed that Creation was placed here for us to eat and wear, and all we had to do was find out how God intended us to use its lower elements. But were they really so businesslike, these ancestors of ours? Surely well-treated cats were no less affectionate, kittens no less endearing, and there were children a thousand years ago, and monks, nuns, widows, prisoners, sailors, and people in isolated hamlets and fortresses who may have needed affection as much as rodent control.

We can't know. After Egypt the cat begins to slip underneath history, at knee level. In feudal times the master's favorite hawks, hounds, and horses all had their quarters, and the Great Hall was heaped with snoozing dogs; where was the cat? Was an individual cat a farm tool rather than a friend, out in the stable treading a nest for kittens in the hay? Or was it asleep on the mistress's bed? Or in the kitchen watching the meat turn on the spit?

Probably it was better off in England than in northern Europe. In 1205, the English Nuns' Rule stated, "Ye shall not possess any beast, my dear sisters, except only a cat." In the fourteenth century, Chaucer wrote, "Or take a cat, nourish it well with milk/And tender meat, make it a couch of silk . . ." English etiquette books of the fourteenth and fifteenth centuries forbade the feeding of cats under the table. Certainly some cats were appreciated as much for themselves as for their granary work.

There's a great psychological gulf between corn crib and lap, between farmhand and friend, and very few of our useful creatures have taken the leap, or wanted to. Probably many cats didn't. Certainly some did. Came inside, small and with cleanly habits, perhaps looking for a safer place to kitten, and looked into people's eyes and purred when touched, and stayed. Or were brought in, because of being lame or sickly or orphaned, and cosseted by the kitchen fire, and stayed. Whoever made the first move, cat or human, probably people far from Egypt became attached to their cats then as they do now, mice or no mice.

The surviving written word concerns itself with practical matters. For instance, the Welsh king Hywel Dda in 936 organized the tribal laws that had been established by long custom. A newborn kitten's value, or the compensation payable to its owner if you killed it, was one cent. When its eyes had opened it was worth two cents, and after it had killed its first mouse it was worth four cents, which would also buy you a sheep or a goat. To clarify the matter for barter, a calf, an ordinary filly, and a cat were of equal worth, unless the cat was one of the many that watched the king's own granaries and so worth a lot more. If you stole one of the king's cats, the fine was a pile of grain equal to the length of the cat, including its tail. The cat was held up by the tail and grain heaped around to its full length, which can't have done either the cat or the tail holder any good.

In order to enjoy legal status as a hamlet, a Welsh settlement had to include nine buildings, a plow, a kiln, a churn, a bull, a cock, a herdsman, and a cat.

If husband and wife separated, the wife got the cat.

Clearly the cat was a person of consequence in farming country, a creature with a legal position, and worth stealing. But no document mentions its emotional status. No one bothered to record that in the year 400, or 600, or 1000, such-and-such a fisherman or shepherd or farmwife dearly loved an old striped tom with a torn ear.

It seems likely that they did, though, and even continued to do so through the dark times that lay ahead.

7

Cats and the Church

The cat is useful for catching mice, and affectionate toward affectionate people, but there's something else, something odd about the cat, something more than meets the eye. Everyone's noticed it.

The cat, always and everywhere, has been a means of getting in touch with something unreachable by humans—the Egyptian Land of the Dead, the Norse World Serpent at the bottom of the sea, the future, the Christian Hell, spirits good and bad, and uncontrollable factors like the weather, love, shipwrecks, and wealth. A cat has always been what the computer people call a "communications tool."

In one of the sections in *A Certain Lucas*, Julio Córtazar announces his realization, in the middle of a business meeting, that cats are telephones, cordless telephones, who have been trying since antiquity to communicate messages to their biped subscribers. Unfortunately, even if humans do discover that the cat is indeed a telephone, we have no way of understanding the message it has to convey or its origin, but the cat continues to try. Sometimes its silken discourse and sentences as smooth as glycerine concern hunger, at which times the cat is simply a cat, but at other times the cat has no personal needs to explain and is speaking purely as a telephone from elsewhere. "Clumsy and pretentious, we have let milennia go by without answering the calls, without wondering where they were coming from or who was on the other end of that line which a twitching tail grew tired of showing us in houses all over the world."

A stable and self-confident society can take a few domestic animals walking around like open lines to another world; a society in transition is touchier. A society of innumerable major and minor deities among which the citizens may pick and choose can take their come-and-go in stride, but monotheistic Christianity, jealously exclusive, marched across Europe hand in hand with patriarchy and brought bad news for cats, goddesses, and the unofficial mysteries.

In the fourth century the Emperor Constantine established Christianity as the state religion of a good deal of the civilized world. His nephew, Julian the Apostate, made a rebellious effort to restore pagan tolerance, but it didn't last; after his death his heirs decreed uniform Christianity and launched the long campaign to stamp out competition. The Roman Empire fell, but the Christian empire grew and spread.

At the same time, in Arabia, Mohammed was building up another monotheistic religion, but this was a less ominous one for cats. The Koran stated that while dogs were unclean creatures, cats were the very essence of purity. At Bab-el-Nasz a cat hospital was established, and contributing food to its patients was an act of piety. Cats were most especially never to be chased out of the mosque. In a recent television program on Islamic Africa, rows of the white-robed faithful are prostrating themselves in the mosque as a fine striped cat with white gloves strolls past the camera and on beside their bowed heads, tail on high and fluttering with confidence, a traditionally welcome guest.

Christianity's specific horror of cats came on slowly and sporadically. In the sixth century Pope Gregory the Great had a cat he was deeply attached to, and Saint Jerome kept a cat as well as his more famous lion. Saint Agatha, back in the third century, was a kind of patron saint of cats, though she may have inherited a sanitized version of an older cat cult; her day is February 5, and in later centuries cats found abroad in the month of February were considered witches, and killed.

Moving across Europe, the Church wrestled everywhere with the entrenched customs of paganism. Under pressure, they were to fragment and go underground, and debased forms of them, still connected with animals, resurfaced everywhere as sorcery and diabolism.

Northern Europe, which had maintained contact with Egypt through the Amber Trade Route since a thousand years before Christ, worshiped a major goddess named Freya (or Freyia, Frieda, Feyda, Frigga, Freja, or Frigg), with noticeable overtones of Bastet. In Greenland, women worshiping Freya wore gloves of white catskin with the fur side inside, a haunting glimpse of white-gloved *libyca* back in the homeland of sacred cats.

Freya was originally a three-way goddess, in charge of sex, motherhood, and destruction, with the power to give and take away life, and the cat was closely associated with her in all these aspects. In the early Norse mythology her chariot was pulled by two cats, and by the fifteenth century in Scotland their numbers had increased, as cats' numbers will, to twenty. Gradually her motherhood jurisdiction withered away and left her with the two opposing aspects of sex and destruction, of love and marriage and of disease and death. She was the foremost of the Valkyries, and she and her cats prowled the battlefields deciding who would die, and escorted them to her underworld.

On the other hand, Friday was the preferred day to get married because, being her sacred day, it promised fertility: Freya was always promiscuous. In the myths she had affairs with most of the male gods, and her festivals were public orgies that may have seemed more prurient in the iron-gray north than under the blue skies of the beneficent Nile. What the Church could not abolish it tried to adopt, but it found no equivalent to Freya. She and her cats were clearly unassimilable in the new religion, and a basic and surprisingly durable enemy.

The Church had better luck absorbing other matters. The

two main celebrations of the pagan year, the winter and summer solstices, were converted to the respective birthdays of Christ and John the Baptist, but they brought with them to their new respectability their raucous old ceremonies, dancing, feasting, games, improper songs, and bonfires. Regrettably, some of the bonfires were made of live cats.

The cat's association with fertility had always been a mixed blessing for the cat; cat sacrifices in the interests of a good crop had sprung up in many cultures. With the absorption of pagan practice into Christian ceremony the custom flourished under new auspices, and the Church set up official cat-burnings of its own to underline the message that these were basically Christian, not pagan, occasions and had nothing to do with crop magic.

The druids seem to have patented the wicker cage that held live cats over the flames, and later iron cages came into fashion for their greater durability, prolonging the excitement, but more casual sacrifice needed only a good fire and some cats.

Cats were burned alive at the beginning of spring, which was now called Lent, or buried alive in the fields to protect the crop from evil spirits. In southwestern France a kitten would be buried alive to clear the weeds from a patch of ground, a horticultural practice I can't recommend as I don't think it would work, and cats were buried alive around apple trees to increase the yield, which might indeed work. In Russia, Poland, and Bohemia a black cat was buried alive in the freshly plowed fields. Shrove Tuesday and Lent's first Sunday were popular occasions for burning cats, but on all Lenten Sundays and Wednesdays it was especially pleasing in the eye of Heaven, culminating in some areas in an enormous Easter Sunday cat fire. In Denmark a live cat was put in a barrel on the eve of Shrove Tuesday, and horsemen tilted at the barrel with spears to run it through. In parts of England a cat had to be whipped to death on Shrove Tuesday, and in Roxburghshire one was put in a barrel of soot and the barrel beaten with sticks until it fell apart; the maddened cat, trying to escape, was caught and killed by the excited crowd.

Perhaps the most successful Lenten ceremony, Cat Wednesday, took place in France, at Metz. Held on the second Wednesday in Lent, it was first mentioned in 962, not long after King Hywel Dda had established the high value of Welsh cats and Henry I of Saxony had decreed a fine of fifty bushels of corn for killing a cat. Cat Wednesday became the heart of a famous festival that continued until 1773, with a grand bonfire attended by the governor and chief magistrate; all the civil and military authorities helped in the burning of thirteen cats in a wooden cage over a fire while everyone danced. The cats were said to be disguised witches, and this seems to be the first definite mention of cats in connection with anti-Christian sorcery. Worse was to come.

Midsummer, now called the Eve of St. John, occasioned the greatest cat fires of the year, and the most persistent; the event wasn't discontinued in the province of Meurthe until 1905. In Paris great numbers of cats were packed into a barrel or basket and swung from a pole over a roaring fire in the Place de Greve; afterward people took home scraps of ash and scorched bone for good luck and protection from lightning. A specialized vocation was the collecting of cats for the fire, and the record shows that a Lucas Pommerieux was paid a hundred Paris sous for supplying, over a period of time ending on St. John's 1573, all the cats "necessary" for the Paris fire plus a large canvas sack to contain them. The king attended the event; in 1648 Louis XIV lit the fire wearing a wreath of roses.

Midsummer still had its unsettling ambiguities, though. At Aix-en-Provence, up until 1757, the area was scoured for the very finest tomcat, who was wrapped in swaddling clothes to represent the infant Jesus, adored at a special shrine, and taken on procession in a litter with flowers strewn in his path. Then at noon on June 24 he was put in a wicker basket and thrown into a large bonfire in the city square, while bishops and priests sang accompanying anthems.

After St. John's, the next important cat event was the harvest, now All Saints' Day. Throughout France and Germany a fine plump cat would be decorated with garlands at the beginning of the growing season and pampered until the harvest, when it was eaten. In France a cat was buried under the last bundle of wheat before it was threshed, and when the threshers' flails had killed it, it was roasted, to be eaten on the following Sunday. It's hinted that even today in remote places a cat is ritually burned alive to celebrate the last of the harvest home, or buried alive at the entrance to the barn; getting in the last of the crops is still called "killing the cat" in some countries. The cat, a male cat here, descended from the Great Cat Ra, had assumed the duties of a kind of corn god, and it had to be propitiated for the next year's growing season by decking it in ribbons and worshiping it, or by killing it, or both.

The effort to assimilate and sanctify the season with All Saints' Day was never entirely successful; the end of October retains an unhallowed air, and the witches of the night before seem more present than the saints of the day. The truth is that Christianity was never as deeply concerned with field crops as the pagan cults were, and had nothing solid to offer as a substitute, so cats continued to be more involved than priests in farming and fertility matters.

Least important for cats was Christmas, and sometimes only a single cat sufficed to celebrate it, usually tied alive to a stake and roasted slowly. In parts of central Europe black tomcats were buried in the fields on Christmas Eve to keep evil spirits away from next year's crops, but in general it was a time of truce until February, when witch-cats associated with Saint Agatha were killed for appearing abroad, perhaps on the assumption that any cat not sensibly in front of the fire at that season must be driven by demonic business. Then it was Lent again.

Throughout the eleventh, twelfth, and thirteenth centuries, the identification of cats with sorcery spread and grew, and the ceremonial nature of cat sacrifice began to degenerate into free-for-all torture. It was never sufficient for the cat merely to die; considerable suffering was part of the point. Cats were burned, boiled, impaled, hanged, skinned alive, gutted alive, buried alive, dropped from towers, stoned, scalded, and stabbed. An added touch to the traditional bonfire was a mast or pole in its center; cats fought each other in the flames to scramble up it to brief safety, extending the ceremony until the last screaming victim fell back to its death. In 1231 Pope Gregory XI set up the Inquisition, and the owners or befrienders of cats, accused of worshiping the devil, were burned as well.

Very likely the cat in Europe would have been completely exterminated during the Middle Ages if it hadn't had an ironically lucky break from the enemy Church itself; returning Crusaders brought back a new kind of rat in their ships, the black rat. This Palestinian import was smarter, hungrier, and more prolific than the few native rats, which it quickly supplanted, and within fifty years it had swept through Europe, spreading plague and destroying as much as half the harvested grain. Cats were badly needed for their ancient purpose in farming areas and around mills; sheer common sense in the countryside saved enough of them to keep the populace from starving and the cat itself from vanishing.

Not all cat killings were connected with the Christian calendar and anti-Christian sorcery. A particular highlight of the coronation of Elizabeth I was the burning of a huge wicker effigy of the Pope, stuffed with live cats to provide appropriate sound effects. Throughout northern Europe and the British Isles cats somehow retained their benign connection with hearth and home, so that when you built a house it was wise to bury a live cat under the threshold, and when you moved into a house it was customary to roast a cat on its hearth, to ensure domestic happiness. In the footings of the walls and towers of castles and churches cats were buried alive as guardian spirits and to make sure the building would stand stoutly; even august Westminster, during later repairs, gave up its withered feline body. Cat sacrifices attended the building of bridges; cats were particularly associated with bridges, and all sorts of odd and complicated stories survive about cats and bridges and the devil.

A bright cat would have done well to emigrate from Christendom altogether. Eurocentric scholarship shapes the records, but Buddhists do not torture animals, and Hindus have always been instructed to keep and feed at least one cat in the home. In Japan, the killer of a cat was to be cursed by ill fortune for seven generations. The Islamic world kept its traditional respect for cats, and in 1280 the Sultan of Egypt and Syria left provision in his will for a garden for homeless cats, where they were to be freely fed and cared for. Ghet-el-Quoth, it was called, or Orchard of Cats.

It's restful to the mind to turn away from the agonized feline screams of six hundred European years and think of the Orchard, and sleek cats in it lazily watching butterflies in the sunshine, licking their shoulders and looking forward to dinner. The cat will endure, even in Europe, though just barely.

Devil worship in Christendom was not a myth. The Church was not utterly paranoid. It was battling the remains of a tradition from prehistory that found animals spiritually important, and trying to supplant it with an invisible man-like God who paid no attention to the ancient preoccupations of birth and farming and held that only man was possessed of spirit, or soul, or immortality, or any sort of meaningful reality at all. Back in the fourth century, Saint Ambrose had protested that the doctrine of animal soulless-ness was leading to frightful cruelty, but the Church's main concern was its war against pagans, and spiritual animals were a pagan concept. Cats harked back to Freya, whose underground cult was still very much alive. They harked back to pagan preoccupations like fields and sex and weather, and were therefore a direct line to the Devil, his incarnation and representative.

The Devil in the Middle Ages was a main character in life. Everything unexplainable or unlucky or theologically unorthodox was his doing, and in his carvings and drawings he got increasingly ugly. He had cat's ears. He rode on a black cat. Devil cats held dances, and a black cat led them.

The head cat was always black, the color of evil. Witches under torture confessed to worshiping the Devil in the form of a black cat.

Witches were not a myth either. They existed all over Europe, and met in secret covens, and worshiped in bizarre rites that were a surviving corruption of the more formal pagan ceremonies. Cats, especially black cats, were important in their rituals. Goats and cocks were involved on a regular basis too, and authorities point them out as equally demonic, but it's worth noting that nobody held them responsible for their connections; no goat or rooster burnings were recorded. They were victims or accessories; cats were principals.

Men as well as women took part. In 1305 the Archbishop of Coventry was arraigned before the Pope for worshiping the Devil in the form of a cat. He was too important a figure to be burned at the stake, but my own feeling is that he was guilty as charged; you don't accuse an archbishop of Devil worship without *some* evidence.

The fragments of decaying religions, practiced in secret, rot into unpleasant forms. There were complicated sexual orgies, and disagreeable rites in which the elect were allowed to kiss the anus of a black cat, animal blood was used extensively, and peculiar refreshments, like cat soup, were served.

In 1484 Pope Innocent VIII issued a papal bull, "Against Sorcerers," designed to stamp out these rotten scraps of paganism, and the witch hunt gained momentum.

As the modern concept of the witch began to take shape, old and unattractive women became strongly suspect. Spinsters were likely witches because in some of the myths Freya's attendants were virgins. The young and the married were not exempt, however, and many a man turned in his wife for suspected midnight rambles. Dozens of stories tell of women who slipped out of their husbands' beds to take part in diabolic rites, usually having changed their shape to a cat's. It was no longer necessary to own or be seen with a cat, since it was well known that any witch could turn into one simply by rubbing herself with an ointment made from the fat of a black cat. In many of the stories, the errant woman gets hurt while in her cat form. A man or group of men stumbles on the cats at their wicked revels and wounds one, usually in the paw, and in the morning a local woman is seen with a limp or a wounded hand and burned as a witch. (Cats could change themselves into women, too, often for love of a man, but usually betrayed themselves by chasing mice.)

In the sixteenth and seventeenth centuries, over a hundred thousand witches were executed in Germany, and seventy-five thousand in France. America, coming late to the game, convicted a mere two thousand of cat-related witchcraft. The dead cats were long past counting.

The Church found a new ally in the medical profession, which joined enthusiastically in the witch hunt. Witches and sorcerers, when in their human forms, claimed to cure diseases with herbs and spells, and given the state of official medicine at the time were probably safer and more effective than the doctors, who resented the competition.

Basically, any cat might be and probably was a witch, but certain tests could be made. A cat that showed reluctance or alarm when confronted with holy water or a crucifix was a witch, as was any cat that didn't die immediately when you tried to kill it. A cat connected with or seen around a house where there was illness or injury, or even soured milk, was a witch. A cat found near fields where the crops were doing poorly was a witch. Any trouble involving a human baby was witchcraft and a death warrant for the nearest cat. In Hungary all cats between the ages of seven and twelve were sorcerers. A cat near a deathbed was a sorcerer waiting to seize the victim's soul, and a cat near a baby was a witch waiting to kill it by sucking its breath.

Witches and sorcerers had made a contract with the Devil, their souls in return for favors, usually money, making the possession of money questionable in itself (though the lack of it didn't exonerate you; you might have it hidden). The Devil was invoked by various chantings, and appeared in the form of, naturally, a black cat, to work out the agreement by which he would be your servant in exchange for your soul. The contract was signed by a mark on the new witch's body, generally a cat's paw print in blue or red, reminiscent of the guardian cat tattoo in Egypt. This mark was insensitive to pain. Inquisitors looked for it on witches, and if it wasn't visible it could be located by stabbing the suspect all over with needles until, perhaps exhausted, she stopped screaming, which meant the Devil's mark had been found.

The Devil's access to money made him a popular figure to invoke. Pious folk tortured and killed cats to please God, but the impious did it to summon the Devil. Since the cat was his own creature, if he heard its screams of pain he might appear and offer you gold and silver to let it go. He can't have done this very often, but a surprising number of people kept trying. Their faith seems a bit irrational in hindsight, but everyone must have heard of the cousin of a friend of a friend to whom it had actually happened.

The most tiring diabolic invocation appeared in the Scottish highlands. The Devil was to be summoned in the form of an enormous black cat, and the summoners were ordinary black cats. The ceremony began at midnight on Freya's Friday. The supplicant roasted a black cat alive, turning it on a spit, as slowly as possible to prolong the howls of pain. The trick part was that the instant the cat mercifully died and stopped howling it had to be replaced by another black cat, and this procedure had to be carried out over four full days and nights, ninety-six hours, during which the petitioner paused for neither food nor rest; "keep the cat turning," as they still say in the Hebrides. The ritual must have used up an enormous number of cats, no matter how slow the fire. If it was astonishing that cats survived at all, that the black genes endured and there are still black cats around today seems nothing short of miraculous, or perhaps diabolical. The last recorded performance of this rite was undertaken in 1750 by two brothers named Maclean, and according to the record it worked; at the end of the fourth day the huge black cat appeared and gave the brothers wealth and heirs.

It was scarcely necessary to sell the Devil one's soul if he could be blackmailed into doing one's bidding, and the notion was enduringly popular. In York County, Pennsylvania, during a witch alarm in 1929, a newspaper reported that you could bully the Devil into leaving you in peace by plunging a live black cat into boiling water and, having cooked it down, keeping the last bone of its tail as a protective amulet.

The connection of the black cat with money from the Devil lived on more benignly after the Devil had lost his grip; even in the Middle Ages money cats turn up without satanic connections. After all, cats had once been in charge of the prosperity of good crops, so why not the prosperity of cash in a cash society? Puss-in-Boots, who made his master rich beyond imagining, is a tale of ancient and cloudy origins that first surfaced in sixteenth-century Italy, and surely no one doubts that Puss was black. In the fourteenth century Dick Whittington, thrice Lord Mayor of London, doesn't seem to have recorded the color of the cat who made him rich, though contrary to legend he wasn't poor to start with; being real, she may have been a perfectly ordinary gray tabby with a white bib. Stories of cats that bring their masters fortunes go back at least a hundred years before Whittington, in places as far apart as Denmark and Persia. And in parts of twentieth-century France, a kind of godlet black cat is called the matagot, and brings its household great fortune as long as it's always served the first bite of every meal. One version holds that you must keep your matagot cat in a chest, and every morning you will find a gold coin in with it; I suppose if you let it out it would be stolen immediately, and no wonder. In Brittany, the lucky black cat is called a Silver Cat, because he goes out by night and brings home money to his people. He can serve nine masters and make each one rich. (Seven and nine are the cat numbers. Everyone knows they have nine lives, and in Sicily if a black cat serves seven masters it will take the soul of the seventh to hell. In Russia, all black cats turn into the Devil at the age of seven.)

The cat's connections with eyes and seeing, in addition to money, held fast in the underground culture. In *The Once and Future King* T. H. White offers us a recipe used by the sorceress Morgan le Fay. It called, as most such recipes did, for an entirely black cat without a white hair; the cat must be boiled very slowly until all the meat falls from its bones, and a certain small bone, when held in the mouth, makes the cook invisible. In a simpler process from *L'Evangile du Diable* (*The Devil's Bible*), invisibility is produced if you only put the cooked meat in a new dish and throw it over your shoulder.

The flesh, bones, blood, brains, ashes, and fat of black cats all had magical properties. Even the afterbirth was useful; the Talmud offers a complicated long-range plan for seeing evil spirits, in which you take the afterbirth of a black female that is the first-born kitten of a black mother who was also the first-born of her mother, and burn it and rub the ashes in your eyes. In Cornwall, a sty can be cured by stroking your eye with the tail of a black cat, which, mercifully, can remain attached to its owner. Topsell's 1606 *Histoire of Foure-Footed Beastes* has a recipe that cures blindness and all eye diseases with a powder made from the burnt head of a black cat.

On the other hand, if you intend to cheat or steal from someone, the ashes of a blind cat thrown in his eyes will blind him to your plans. In the British Isles if a cat has jumped over a corpse, or even been in a room with one, the next person who sees it will go blind.

If black cats were in charge of black sorcery, it seemed reasonable to some that white cats were good magic, though this didn't always work to their advantage: evil spirits could be warded off by throwing the head and tail of a white cat into the fire.

White cats were always popular in the Orient. In the early Middle Ages in Japan, a whole cat cult grew up out of the mystical occasion when a white cat, imported from

China, produced five white kittens on the tenth day of the fifth moon. They were cosseted like princelings, and the fashion spread. For centuries cats were spoiled and kept indoors or walked on leashes and tempted with delicacies, while mice wrought havoc among the silkworm cocoons. Unsuccessful attempts were made to frighten off the mice with pictures and figurines of cats, until, regretfully, in 1602 decrees were passed sending the cats back to work.

In World War II, when the Allies entered Burma they found the local population hostile after intensive Japanese propaganda until a resourceful British colonel had white cats stenciled on all the Army's jeeps and trucks; the Burmese were so impressed by this powerful talisman that they abandoned their Japanese connections to cooperate with the Allies.

Three-colored cats also enjoy a special position in the East, and Japanese ships have always carried them for their usefulness in predicting storms, succoring the souls of the drowned, and guiding ships to safety.

The cat's sovereignty over storms, weather, and the sea continued. In the British Isles and other seagoing northern countries, shipwrecking storms could be created by throwing cats into the sea. A witch-cat washing its ears could cause thunderstorms; in modern times it still means rain or frost is coming. The way a cat sleeps predicts warm or cold weather, reasonably enough, since even the least clairvoyant cat sprawls when hot and curls when cold. In Java rain can be induced by washing a cat or, better, a pair of cats.

The cat's jurisdiction over matters of sex, marriage, and home life also persisted. In the Middle East black cats have always had aphrodisiac powers. In Europe Freya's lusty powers moved easily from orgies to marriage. A black cat is a lucky wedding present. A girl will be lucky who hears a cat sneeze on her wedding day. A black cat around the house ensures that all the daughters will marry well, but a girl who steps on a cat's tail won't marry for at least a year. In France, it rains on the weddings of those who have mistreated cats, and in the Netherlands it's bad luck if the cat sits by the door on the day of the wedding, meaning it wants to leave because the bride hasn't treated it with proper respect.

So the cat emerged from its centuries of diabolic association and Church persecution with quite a lot of its Egyptian and pagan powers intact. Death and eternity had been taken over by the Church, sickness and health by doctors, and the sun and moon by men with telescopes, but the cat remained the open line to money, crops, eyesight, weather, and sexual and domestic felicity.

Through the sixteenth and seventeenth centuries the cat fires raged, but there were breaks in the gloom here and there. Cardinal Wolsey, who became Henry VIII's lord chancellor in 1515, was powerful enough to keep any pet he pleased, and carried his cat to the dinner table and to the cathedral when he officiated at services. A hundred years later Cardinal Richelieu, chief minister to Louis XIII, had fourteen cats that he was deeply attached to, and let them sit on his desk and play with the wigs of his distinguished visitors. He made generous provision for them in his will, but unfortunately when he died in 1642 his Swiss guards, more typical of their time, collected and burned them all.

In the 1660s in England, Samuel Pepys kept a cat, and was no crosser than the rest of us when he had to get up and let it out at night; nor did he wonder where it was going. It's hard to imagine Pepys dancing around a fire of cats, much less worshiping a cat-shaped devil. He was an educated man of active scientific curiosity, fond of theater and pretty women and making money; his religion was confined to thanking God at the end of every month when he totted up his accounts. A God with a personal interest in one's profit-and-loss ledgers has changed somewhat from One who liked cats burning. Cats still burned, but Pepys was the wave of the future.

It would be nice to think that the Church recognized the error of its ways and absolved the cat of evil, but more likely the torturing of cats was simply, finally, going out of fashion. In the European cities of the late seventeenth cen-

tury, education was becoming less clerical and educated
men more visible. Scientific experiment was a fashionable
hobby; superstition was for country folk, for crones, for the
ignorant and old-fashioned. The pagan threat had withered.
The old gods shriveled into fairies with gauzy wings, wee
folk in funny hats, goblins to be tolerantly ridiculed in
cities; the corn god shrank back into his shrinking fields.
Like witches, these rural sprites can still do mischief if displeased, but it's a mild bucolic mischief, souring milk or
borrowing your horse by night and bringing it home
muddy. Although these gods have become quite separated
from the feline, it's still taken for granted everywhere that
they can be placated and made into useful guardian spirits
with regular saucers of milk or porridge left on the kitchen
floor or on the doorstep by night.

The cat and the Devil were parting company, and by the
middle of the eighteenth century Christopher Smart could
write:

For I will consider my cat Jeoffry.
For he is the servant of the Living God, duly and daily
    serving him.
For he keeps the Lord's watch in the night against the
    Devil, who is death, by brisking about the life.
For in his morning orisons he loves the sun and the sun
    loves him.
For he is of the tribe of Tiger.
For the Cherub Cat is a term of the Angel Tiger.
For he has the subtlety and hissing of a serpent, which in
    goodness he suppresses.
For he will not do destruction, if he is well-fed, neither will
    he spit without provocation.
For he purrs in thankfulness, when God tells him he's a
    good Cat.

Of course Smart can hardly be considered typical, since
he was an alcoholic, and insane, and at the time was locked

up in Bedlam with only Jeoffry for company. Still, no one suggested burning either of them for his sentiments.

Toward the end of the century Dr. Johnson, as sane as Pepys and not a man given to exercise for its own sake, was going out in person to buy oysters for Hodge, lest the servants take a spiteful dislike to the cat from being put to the effort.

By the beginning of the nineteenth century, the cat has so far lost its evil connotations as to be patronized by the likes of Robert Southey, Poet Laureate of England, who burbled, "A kitten is in the animal world what a rosebud is in a garden." The cat may have been relieved not to be made into bonfires, but one can imagine a quick twitch of irritation at the tip of the tail for being called a rosebud.

Cats were in for a sentimental spell. True, Baudelaire in midcentury wrote respectfully in *Fleurs du Mal*:

> *Stretched pensively in noble attitudes,*
> *Like sphinxes dreaming in their solitudes,*
> *He seems to ponder in an endless trance;*
> *With magic sparks his fecund loins are filled,*
> *And, like fine sand, bright golden atoms gild*
> *With vague and starry rays his mystic glance.*

But Baudelaire was French. In Victorian times a suffocating wave of coziness settled over the English-speaking world, all mysteries lost their darkness, and the cat became as tame as a teapot and, to judge from the paintings, shaped rather like one. Saucers of cream and the company of women and children became its lot; no parlor scene was complete without an overfed cat. Kittens played with balls of yarn. Pretty girls fondled them. We descend from Jeoffry, servant of the Living God and term of the Angel Tiger, to

> *I like little pussy,*
> *Her coat is so warm,*
> *And if I don't hurt her*

She'll do me no harm.
So I'll not pull her tail,
Nor drive her away,
But pussy and I
Very gently will play.

The fierce and lordly Ra-cat had become a young lady, Freya's lusts had been sanitized into family life, and even the valuable hunting instincts had fallen into disrepute; it was considered not quite nice of cats to kill, a deplorable sideline to their proper role as cuddly toys on lap and cushion. Since neutering was uncommon, one wonders how the always noisy and explicit personal sex life of the cat fit into the parlor portrait; nothing is more educational for the young to observe than the magic sparks of those fecund loins, and nothing was less appealing to Victorians than sex education.

We may safely assume that the cat was no cozier in 1880 than it was diabolical in 1380; the cat is not malleable to human opinion. In the Middle Ages when it got the chance it sat on laps; in the nineteenth century when it got the chance it howled on rooftops and ripped open mice.

The twentieth century has been a mixed bag. Veterinary medicine sprang up from virtually nowhere, and eventually turned its attention to cats and began to distinguish their diseases from those of dogs. Vaccines were developed against the great killers like feline enteritis, though they're no use unless someone pays to have them actually administered to the individual cat. Antibiotics arrived for the same privileged few. Cat food, at first an unwholesome, inadequate brew of ground fish scraps, caught the eye of commercial enterprise and improved, and the domestic cat's previous diet of cold noodles, applesauce, fat, and gristle, scraped from a plate, passed into history for the lucky; whole books were to be written on cat nutrition.

On the other side of the balance, the twentieth century brought the car.

The car has changed the cat's life as much as it has our

own, killed far more than the Inquisition, and made prisoners of cared-for cats in populous areas. Signs are taped up on every post and wall: LOST. Missing since 9/3. Gray and white tabby. Orange tabby. All black female with flea collar. Answers to Rusty, Samantha, Tuffy, Tigger, Angela . . . Reward. Owner heartbroken. Child grieving. Large reward, call any time.

Cats that can find their way across the continent are not likely to get lost around the corner; cars have done for Rusty and Samantha, Tuffy and Tigger, as they went about their catly business and refreshed their ancient spirits under the moon that used to be theirs.

Here in the city my cats are prisoners. No more the smells of evening or the joys of the chase, no more trees to climb, bushes to nap under, holes to dig, or even strolls down the alley in search of friendship or a fight. The books all say it's best. The books all say cats adjust to it perfectly well and never miss freedom, learn to watch the world from a window and go to bed at night domestic as a hen.

They're healthy here, and as safe as cats can be. They have each other, and they're fond of me, which may be some compensation, if cats think in terms of compensation, but who can doubt that they're diminished? Did they come this far, having been worshiped as gods, having saved the world from rats, having survived European Christianity, in order to be ornaments for my couch? The old ones sleep more here; there's only dinner to wake up for. Morgan paces and whines and searches my face for the answer.

I think about living in a place where cars are as rare as ostriches, and opening the door, and the cats departing one by one across the garden with their tails up, toward the dark woods where only cats and owls can find their way, swaggering like the cat that walked by its wild lone through scent-scapes of night and rustlings in the grass.

Here we are in the city, though, and everywhere I go along the streets cats behind glass watch me from their windowsills, many of them alone in there all day, and certainly many more without even access to a window and only the motionless furniture to watch. A square of sunlight creeping across the rug. Their minds must be dulled and fogging over, and their spirits shriveling.

Cats are not likely to outlast the car, but cars are not likely to outlast the cat, either, only limit the lives of some and shorten the lives of others. Shortening the lives of strays is a mercy, but the car isn't going to wipe them out. Nothing will.

The underworld of cats will continue, thanks to their resolute sex life and skill and devotion as mothers. All over the world in their millions cats still slip past the hazards of history and between the ankles of adversity and survive, even if only for a year or two, tenacious of life, searching out what they need to stay alive for long enough to nurse their young. And in the intervals of survival, they find a sunny ledge on which to wash, and contract the pupils of their eyes to slits, drawing the iris like a luminous silk curtain almost closed across what it is they know.

There's a notion common to many cultures that you can tell the time by looking into a cat's eyes. Baudelaire looked into his cat's eyes and said: "Yes, I see the time; it is eternity."

8

A Choice of Cats

Not so many years ago in America, the purebred cat was considered a snobbish and specialized taste. Even the word *purebred* was suspect, and smacked of an elitist European reverence for aristocracy. These weren't real cats, they were designer cats, man-made cats, interior decorator cats, probably fragile and neurotic, owned by a small band of fanatics who exhibited them in shows and a larger group who acquired and discarded them according to the color of their furniture. Among the rank and file there was a distinct feeling that they were artificial somehow, created by genetic meddling to please the kind of show-offs who shouldn't be allowed to keep cats in the first place.

It's true that some of the breeds have been produced or at least encouraged by meddling, crosses like the Himalayan, and genetic sports like the Scottish Fold that would have been absorbed again by nature if we hadn't found them interesting. But the major types we've all heard of are natural breeds, just Eastern rather than Western, and no more artificial than an Oriental human. In their early days in the West the small genetic pool may have deepened mental and physical flaws, but bolstered by imports and widely established now they aren't any more fragile and neurotic than the rest of us.

Cats, like women, should be respected as individuals rather than admired as decoration, but there's no harm, given a choice, in taking up with a strikingly attractive specimen of either.

A long time ago, I drove across the United States with a Siamese cat and drew incredulous crowds in the small towns and crossroads where I stopped for gas; many gapers refused to believe it was a cat at all. No one would be surprised to see one now, but a certain suspicion persists. The Siamese is widely considered to be unfriendly, perhaps because of its voice, and neurotic, possibly insane; everyone has a tale of a mad Siamese.

The Siamese is different from other cats, or, since generalization is dangerous and some Siamese are dull as clay, *most* Siamese are different. More intense. They're generally conceded to be highly intelligent, but many people do not feel intelligence is an advantage in a pet. It makes them uncomfortable. Not every Siamese is a genius, either. I had one once with the brains of a potted plant. Son of champions, he had trouble locating his breakfast dish every morning, and spent a lot of time sitting bolt upright in corners with his eyes crossed, apparently trying to remember his own name. In general, though, whatever we mean by intelligence in a cat, they do seem well endowed with it, and the French statesman Poincaré said his Siamese Gri-Gri was "as intelligent as any man."

Properly treated, Siamese develop a deep, single-hearted devotion to their people and overreact to competition, absences, and infidelity like an adolescent in love. They need attention, and think nothing of pulling the books out of the bookcase and the pictures off the walls to get it. They demand notice in a raucous, echoing voice that many people and some other cats find alarming; the sound has been compared to that of a giant sea gull in distress. Taking on a Siamese is rather like getting married.

Show cats are rewarded for being "typey," or slightly more like whatever they are than the next cat. The Siamese is supposed to be a long slender cat with a wedge-shaped head and a thin pointy tail, so the breeders keep working toward longer, slenderer cats with wedgier heads and thinner tails, and the results have come to look something like ferrets. The best Siamese in a cat show is one you could pull through a wedding ring; I'm sure they're perfectly charming cats personally, but they don't look very cozy. For those of us not planning on the show circuit, there's a kind of Siamese underworld. The second- and third-class and no-class Siamese, found in disreputable places like casual classified ads and supermarket bulletin boards and small family catteries and even, if we're a bit wary and inspect carefully, pet shops, are generally considered disreputable indeed. From the better breeders, they're called "pet quality," meaning they're good enough for the likes of you and me but not something a breeder wants hanging around lowering the tone of the neighborhood. They're less serpentine. Their heads are too wide, their eyes too round, and they harbor endearing small imperfections in their tailbones, the knobs and kinks all Siamese used to have. In fact, these rejects look much more like the pictures of the first nineteenth-century imports than any modern ribbon winner does. They may even, in middle age, develop a spreading belt line and a double chin, just like ordinary folk. I recommend them. They cost about as much as dinner for two, with wine, in a fairly good restaurant, and they last longer.

The beginnings of the Siamese are lost in the jungle, and we don't even know for sure which jungle. The *Encyclopedia Americana* thinks they originated in China; the *Britannica* says nothing is known of their ancestry and "there is no living species of Oriental cat that would serve as ancestor."

The sacred cat of Burma is descended from a cat named Sinh the Oracle, who was white but with ears, tail, nose and paws "the color of earth." Its eyes were yellow, but turned blue while it was defending the temple from Siamese invaders, after which all sacred temple cats had blue eyes. This is the long-haired, white-gloved Birman, though, proudly claimed by the Burmese, while what we call Burmese are said to be common in modern Thailand. The Thais say that any Siamese seen in their streets nowadays have been imported from the west, and that *their* cats are Korats, natives of the Korat province there and, though always rare, one of the oldest recorded breeds; they're silver-blue with green or amber eyes. On the other hand, there's a drawing of a seal-point Siamese in The Cat-Book Poems in the Bangkok Museum, and the book came out in 1350.

Jungle boundary lines between countries have never much bothered cats.

The story that arrived in the West with them was that they could be owned only by priests and royalty, and lived jealously guarded in the temples and palaces, and that to steal one was punishable by death. Early imports often had crossed eyes and kinked tails, attributed to watching over temple treasures, staring fixedly at them and wrapping their tails around them for safekeeping. They're said to have attacked thieves. Perhaps they merely spoke, and frightened them off; perhaps they jumped onto their shoulders. Siamese have always liked shoulders. In a Victorian photograph of a pioneer Siamese collector, one of her overweight cats is draped awkwardly but contentedly over her shoulder. Siamese find it amusing to come quietly up behind you and spring from the ground to your shoulder or, failing that, your back, where they hang suspended from your clothes and flesh. Corvo gives a little cry of warning before he jumps; Morgan doesn't. Once settled, they will ride happily around on you, purring with satisfaction and nipping your ear and jaw in the sharp Siamese way of saying "love." Certainly this would disconcert a burglar, but the cats do it only to intimate friends.

Or maybe they tripped the temple thieves; tripping is another Siamese trait. They enjoy pushing ahead of you on the stairs and then hunkering down on the bottom step to see if you will fall over them, the Siamese notion of a joke. Corvo in his wild youth used to trip cars; he lurked in the woods by the road until the car was almost level with him and then danced giddily across in front of it. After he finally succeeded, and lived to tell the tale, he quit.

Perhaps there's nothing but public-relations hype behind the sacred-temple-cat, royalty-only story; at a thousand turn-of-the-century dollars per kitten, the least a buyer could expect was an exotic romance to go with it.

Whoever they were originally, our Siamese did come from Siam. The first pair arriving in England were brought from Bangkok in 1884 by a Mr. Owen Gould; he had been consul-general there, and they were a gift from the king. Their names were Pho and Mia and their kittens won prizes at the Crystal Palace Exhibition in 1885, the same year Miss Forestier-Walker brought in Susan and Tian O'Shian, and the French resident minister in Siam sent a pair to the Jardin des Plantes in Paris, which probably lacked the right emotional atmosphere. The kittens were proving tricky to raise, and enteritis losses were heavy.

In 1900 Mrs. Clinton Locke of Chicago registered Lockhaven Siam and Lockhaven Sally Ward, and the following year she signed up two chocolate points.

All the immigrants carried the genes for chocolate points, with its lighter body color, and the elegantly pale blue point; a blue point named Rhoda was registered in England in 1894. The recessive blue color is said to have been introduced by an all-blue jungle cat of Malaysia, a cross that was entirely the cat's idea. Two seal points with recessive blue genes will produce one blue for every three seal kittens. Blue and chocolate together produce some lilac points, and lilac to lilac will breed true.

All real cats.

Breeding out to plain cats, known as European cats in Europe and American shorthairs in America, has produced some offbeat points like red and tabby, considered Siamese in England and Colorpoint Shorthairs in America. The English seem to go in for more vivid colors than the Americans, and in their pictures the English red points are a startingly fiery red-orange and their blue points almost blue, rather than the dove color common here.

It seems to me there's a temperamental difference between the male and female Siamese, rather like the difference I imagine between lion and lioness. The male is lordly and swaggering and pleased with himself, laid back in his life-style and grandly demanding in his affections; he strolls into a room and expects to be applauded, he stretches in the sun with admiration of his splendid self. When living at home with his own female, he takes a nobly tolerant interest in his kittens and an affectionate, if casual, pride in their accomplishments.

The females, like lionesses, are busy and responsible and fussy, and behave like loving but competent secretaries constantly reminding you of appointments. Morgan cries to be let into my desk drawers to sort through my papers, and keeps a close eye on the other cats and their health and behavior, and rounds them up in time for meals. She wants me out of bed on the tick of seven and back in it again at eleven, and paces back and forth across my book muttering discontentedly if I linger. Corvo thinks I'm well enough the way I am; Morgan is half distracted trying to whip me into shape. She is, however, a tireless and conscientious nurse to ailing man or beast, and would have made a model mother.

Siamese are considered among the best warriors and ratters, and kill snakes too; it's a pity more of them don't have an outdoors. They suffer very much from boredom in small spaces. It isn't a question of exercise, they always get plenty of that; they just long for the unexpected, the new, the odd encounter, the changing scene. Sameness gnaws at them.

Several sources claim that they don't get along with other breeds. This libel probably arose from their jealous passion for their people; the Siamese may have his problems, but he's no snob, as legions of half-breeds will testify. Indeed, the Siamese is a genetic factor in a whole swarm of breeding inventions: Balinese, Bombay, Colorpoint Shorthair, Havana Brown, Himalayan, Lilac Foreign Shorthair, Si-Rex, Manxamese, Oriental Shorthair, and Tonkinese. He enjoyed every minute of it.

Occasionally I see evidence in my two of a vague sense of kinship, and the younger will sometimes watch the older to see what he does so she can do it too, but they seem equally fond of the others.

The Siamese female goes into heat oftener and stays in it longer than anyone else, and makes an unendurable noise about it. Screaming, writhing, and prowling, she bellows with rage at the unarriving prince and wears herself down to the bone with exhaustion; neighbors, even quite distant neighbors, call the police. Her gestation period is longer than a house cat's, and her litters smaller. The kittens are tiny, pure white, and look like larvae. Often their eyes are half open at birth, but in other ways they're slow to develop and need a long childhood.

Siamese cats have been known to eat wool; I heard of one that ate a couch. One theory is that the lanolin in the wool reminds them of the scent around their mother's nipples, and it seems reasonable to guess that the wool eaters left home too young.

In the dark, blue Siamese eyes burn red as rubies instead of green or gold.

I can't leave the Siamese without considering that nameless breed of black cat usually associated with Siamese blood. It is not recognized. Officially, there is no such cat, and those of us who have known one, and we are surprisingly numerous, constitute an exclusive underground cat club, nameless by necessity. We refer to them as *those* cats, as in, "Oh, you have one of *those* cats! I had one once."

There's a recognized cat called the Oriental Shorthair, billed as a knowledgeable blend of Siamese, American Shorthair, Colorpoint Shorthair, and other judicious ingredients, and it comes in exotic colors like Silver and Cameo Smoke, but that's not what we're talking about at all. The cats under consideration are black, and accidental. One source refers to a "royal cross," a splendid black sometimes produced from careful Siamese/Burmese mixing. That's not it either. I had a black Siamese/Burmese cross once, and she was so abysmally dull I finally got rid of her. Jean

Cocteau adored a cat, "a kind of black semi-colon," the grandchild of his Siamese and his blue Persian, but that can't be it either.

Most owners of the magic black cats take it for granted that they're half or part Siamese, but in not one single case have I found a person who could prove it or even reasonably assume it. On the contrary; both my daughter and I, on unrelated occasions, found black kittens born to Siamese mothers and seized on them as certain to be those cats, and both grew up to be as ordinary as cats can be. The magic blacks are all changelings in the cradles of commoners. They come from the shelters; they come in off the streets, ripping furiously at the back door and shouting for admission; they are born among ordinary kittens. The little black cat who lives here now was born in a section of the country where no Siamese genes could be supposed to float among the population; dog and horse country, where any human owning a Siamese would be stoned clear to the county line. Her mother is a dumpy, fluffy, round-faced little person in gray stripes; she herself is one of those cats.

They stand out in a litter. Their ears are large and open, with a bald patch running down to the eyes, and their tails are long and thin. At an age when other kittens look like stuffed toys, they look like six pieces of oiled black string. They seem to mature early. The expression on their faces is extraordinary. They stare into your eyes with peculiar intensity, as if recognizing you in some more penetrating way than you have ever been recognized before. If this is a common mutation or a throwback to an extinct wild type, and if it's been around for a while, no wonder the Church chose the black cat as a supernatural emissary. Whether or not they're interested in buying your soul, they're certainly looking straight into it.

I went to the SPCA to get myself a kitten, and was shown a cage full of them, dozens of them napping and washing and wrestling together. Only one noticed me, and gave a piercing shriek, and climbed the wire of the cage to get as close as possible to my face, screaming all the while and staring steadily into my eyes with that extraordinary recognizing look: where had I been, what had kept me so long? I fell over myself in haste, apologizing, to get the attendant to let him out. That was Boy.

Those cats are exceptionally alert, brave, bossy, curious, and agile, and figure out ways to get into trouble that never occurred to the other cats in the house. They're clever with their hands, and use their mouths as an extra hand. While still quite small they take over the sacred places of the other cats. They eat like young wolves and get longer and heavier but no rounder; their flesh has a hard, spare, uncuddly quality, lean as cheetahs but weighing like bricks. When the baby fluff gives way to proper fur they look like wrought iron and shine like polished coal. Sitting up straight they have the long back and peaked breastbone of Egyptian statues. Their paws are small ovals on which they balance down the path like tightrope walkers.

With the right person, when they grow up they develop an exclusive, passionately possessive relationship, not always demonstrative but unmistakable. It's risky to leave them for long periods and criminal to give them away. Laps are not their milieu; they lie on the chest and neck and bite the chin, or simply sit and look at you. To other members of the family they're barely civil.

Sometimes the object of their love proves unworthy. I met a woman at a party, and we fell to talking of those cats. She had one; it had been her constant companion for six years, until she got another cat. When the new cat came, the black cat went down to the boiler room in the cellar and stayed there. The woman hopes she will die soon, as it's a nuisance going down there in the musty dark to feed it and change the litter. It's been eight years.

To the Siamese cat person the Persian is bland; to the Persian person the Siamese is noisy, demanding, and neurotic. Persians are noninvasive, and never shout. While the Siamese is bellowing for your attention, springing onto your shoulder and biting your cheek to get noticed, the Persian simply pats at your arm, over and over and over, and looks pained. They're gentle, though not nearly as gentle as they look: round eyes and long fur impress people immediately as the essence of gentleness, though the genetic connection would be hard to work out. People who dislike cats or are slightly afraid of them like Persians. Strong, great, lumbering men come to my house carrying refrigerators and such on their backs, and pause nervously on seeing the other cats. Then, on seeing Barney, snow-white and blue-eyed, they melt at once; now, there's a cat they could like. A *gentle* cat. From the emphasis, you'd think the average shorthair was a leopard balanced on the branch overhead.

Actually, even without claws Barney has strong jaws and sharp teeth and can use them to good effect when needed. When he was first mine, and we lived together in a ground-floor apartment, he attacked a police dog he thought was trespassing. The back door was accidentally ajar; the dog, attached to a policeman, was patrolling the alley, and Barney shot out and sprang on him without hesitation. I rushed after him; dog and policeman were both in shock. I apologized, I tried to detach Barney, and he turned and bit deeply into my hand. He was sorry about it, of course, but I was interfering in his guard duties.

Other cats aren't fooled by those cream puff looks. A friend of mine in difficulties parked her cat, an enormous black tom named Butcher, on me while she straightened out her life. Barney knew at once that this wasn't an addition to the family, only a passing guest. He never growled or hissed at Butcher, he never raised a paw, he simply sat on the bottom step of the staircase that led to the room where he and I slept and he looked at Butcher with his round pale eyes, and Butcher understood. The message was that Butcher could stay, as long as he stayed under the couch in the living room. All the way under the couch, out of sight. Since the litter pan was upstairs, and Butcher was under no circumstances to use the stairs, when he needed toilet facilities he could creep out at night while Barney was asleep and use the flowerpots in the kitchen. He could eat, but only if his bowl was shoved under the couch for him. All these instructions passed soundlessly through the air, and Butcher, his whiskers full of dust-mice, obeyed.

Persians are fond of their homes and defend them, don't pine for adventure, and make good apartment cats.

The usual confusion obscures their roots. For a long time, "Angora" was considered a rather ignorant synonym for Persian, but current thinking holds them to be two separate cats, and the Turkish Angora one of the oldest recognized natural breeds, the name being a corruption of "Ankhara," and once the privileged pets of the harems of Constantinople. The Persian is variously claimed to be a mix of Angora and a longhair from Afghanistan, or the descendant of the central Asian Pallas's cat, or manul. One source mentions them in India. Turkey, Persia, Afghanistan, and even the near edge of India spread out in a long contiguous reach, and nationality can't have made much difference to native long-haired cats prowling through the centuries looking for mice and sex. Perhaps what we've come to consider local varieties would depend on what was locally admired, and cherished, and bred. Which king's harem took a fancy to which type.

Longhairs appeared in Europe in the late 1500s. Cardinal Richelieu, in the early 1600s, had an elegant black one named Lucifer among his feline retinue at court. The usual stories about Eastern royalty came with them, and if there wee originally two distinct types they were freely mixed after they came west.

Concerned about the purity of what they felt was the true Angora type, officials at the zoo in Ankhara recently undertook a breeding program with several pairs in what they felt was the authentic color, pure white, with blue or amber eyes. It was from these that an American army colonel brought back two pairs in the early 1960s, and breeders are working from their descendants. This authenticated Angora is longer and slenderer than the Persian, and its head is quite different, wedge-shaped, with a long foxy nose, slanted eyes, and big pointed ears. It carries its tail up over its back.

The Persian, on the other hand, is square and solid, deep-chested and short-legged, with short ears and nose on a big square head. It has big round eyes and an expression defined by some as "sweet" and by others as "mournful" or "imperious." The extremest type, the peke-faced, with a nose so short it's said to have trouble breathing, must have its admirers, though I can't think why.

The assertive, inquisitive, imaginative breeds enjoy a reputation for brains. It's harder to tell with the sedate Persian, but the ease with which Barney understood his new uncaged life at the age of ten speaks well for him. Curiosity may be a sign of intelligence, but contentment shouldn't be considered stupidity.

Dignified and affectionate, well-behaved and a bit lazy, the Persian has only two drawbacks: it seldom provides its owner with funny stories to tell at dinner parties, and it sheds. Some shed more than others. Friends of mine have a dark tortoiseshell with coarse, full-bodied fur that stays with her; she rarely has mats of hairballs, and doesn't create housekeeping and dry-cleaning problems. Barney's weightless fluff seems to be everywhere but on Barney in every month of the year. Where it does stay on him, it makes mats; he needs brushing and vacuuming. He much enjoys being vacuumed, and rushes over when I turn the thing on; it's one of his few pleasures now. Confined to quarters here, he sleeps a lot.

A Persian looks dramatic, but there's nothing dramatic about his temperament, and he wouldn't be first choice for people looking for an exciting relationship and major personage in their lives. He's a fine choice, though, for those of us busy and away a lot. He'll wait, and be glad to see us when we do get home, unlike Siamese, who, when we come back, rage and sulk until it's time for us to leave again, and Abyssinians, who will have dismantled our closets and pulled all the papers out of our drawers and probably made a lot of long-distance calls on our bill.

* * *

What's called a Himalayan in these parts and a Colorpoint Longhair in England and a Khmer in France is just what it looks like, a blend of Siamese and Persian. Why, you may ask, when we already have the ancient and sturdy originals, each with its own distinct character, muddle around with a mix of the two and satisfy the aficionados of neither?

A.C. Jude, in an older book, *Cat Genetics*, called them merely, "interesting," speaking as a geneticist, and doubted they would ever become popular. He was wrong.

They have been said to be delicate, perhaps due to inbreeding; one authority mentions a sixty percent mortality rate. Their fanciers say they have the sweet dispositions of Persians, though in this case we may have sweetness confused with imbecility. The only thing Siamese about them is the coloring. The few I've known seem shy and rather tentative, as if astonished by themselves, and why not? On the map we can see the unbridgeable miles between their two homelands; this isn't a blend they could have thought up for themselves, and they seem uncomfortable with it.

A breeder friend of mine had trouble with her Himalayan stud, who was chastely in love with his sister and had eyes for no other. Perhaps he was doing his bit to put a stop to the whole experiment. Just because a thing can be done doesn't mean it ought to be done.

Off the record, cat professionals warn against the taut and elegant Abyssinians. It's their ceaseless busyness; it makes them hard to manage. They pull the stitches out of their incisions and unfasten their splints and bandages. They take the house apart piece by piece and leap easily onto the curtain rods. "It gave me a headache just watching them," said an anonymous breeder. "Made me want to go and lie down."

Going and lying down is what they don't do. If part of the purpose of other cats is to teach us the blessing of peacefulness, the lesson of the Aby is industry.

A wide body of belief holds them to be the direct lineal descendants of the sacred kaffir cats of Egypt. One source says they were brought to England from Abyssinia, now Ethiopia, by returning British soldiers in the 1860s; another says firmly that they're unknown in Abyssinia. The English writer Grace Tabor, who wrote a book about her Aby Amber, says the Phoenicians originally took them to Egypt.

Another writer plainly considers them non-domesticus and says, a bit dubiously, that they have been tamed in parts of Europe.

They don't look tamed.

The distinctive thing about the Abyssinian is its ticked fur. Each hair is ruddy brown or red (or, now, blue) for three quarters of its length, and then ticked at the end with a double or triple bar. The underparts are solid cream or tawny. The ears are tufty. Altogether the effect is far from domesticated, the kind of creature that, if you saw it in the woods, would make you hold your breath and inch foward, careful not to startle it, to get a closer look.

They're generally considered to be the closest domestic cat (if you believe they're domestic cats) to the authentic, ancient, wild original (if you believe there was once a single original). Tabor says they've been called water cats, and were used to catch fish back in the dawn of things. They're strongly psychic, and see ghosts. Loving, rather timid, tirelessly curious, they have an uncontrollable passion for secrets, for the half hidden, the half closed, pocketbooks, bureau drawers, briefcases, the insides of cupboards and refrigerators. Flinging things over their shoulders, they rummage with the anxious intensity of a man who has lost something small but priceless in the laundry basket. When you yell at an Abyssinian, it gives you a look of utter, astonished innocence: Abys cannot be blamed.

If you live in close quarters, an Aby will have to keep itself busy by dismantling them. Two Abys will make twice as much mess but entertain each other.

Remember you were warned. They're happy cats, though. To have missed the joy is to have missed all.

Very recently, a cattery in Michigan, looking for an Aby-pointed Siamese in the usual dissatisfied way of catteries, crossed a Siamese and an Abyssinian, bred one of the kittens back to the Siamese, and to their astonishment came up with spots. The spots run horizontally along the cat, not at all like the vertical pattern of interrupted tabby stripes. Much as I disapprove of this kind of tinkering, the Ocicats are dazzling to look at, with the alert, affectionate faces of anyone's favorite puss and the wild spots of something that leaps for the jugular. They're expensive, scarce, and as artificial as possible, but they're certainly electrifying to see. In 1986, the CFA gave them provisional, or wait-and-see, status.

The friends of the brown Burmese insist that no one is more affectionate and loving than a Burmese, and it may be that they are right and I am wrong; stranger things have happened. My own feeling is that it's a question of heat. Burmese are heat freaks. To the standard query "Hot enough for you?" the Burmese answer is no. Burma, if that's really the country we're dealing with here, is famous for its swampy warmth. If the air in your house rarely gets above eighty degrees, and you sit there being ninety-eight point six, you will have a Burmese on your lap, and that Burmese will stay there until the room temperature reaches ninety-nine. If you're trying to work or eat or sleep, you can throw the Burmese on the floor, and it will be back almost before it hits bottom, and you can keep on throwing it till you're sobbing with rage and frustration and still it returns. They're enormously stubborn, and it's impossible to insult them or hurt their feelings; their golden stare defies you to penetrate their self-absorption. By night they sleep heavily across your throat, over the warm pulse point, and give you nightmares.

When the Siamese cat lies down heavily on your person, he is claiming your flesh as his personal property; when the Burmese does, he is warming his feet.

Bossy with other cats, they fret themselves unless clearly top cat, and may develop respiratory diseases if they don't get their own way.

Recently they've started appearing on the market in a rainbow of colors, red, lilac, blue, cream, and so on, which is confusing since their brownness was the point of them to start with, and it's odd to see their boxy little faces looking out from under cream-colored fur.

All American Burmese are descended from Wong Mau, who came from Burma and was taken up by a Dr. Joseph C. Thompson of San Francisco in 1930. With the help of the Siamese, Thompson established the breed. Wong Mau had powerful genes; Burmese are not Siamese at all.

If you want a cat on your lap and in your bed at all times, winter and summer, go Burmese. Don't get two of them, though; they will ignore you and sleep with each other, because a cat's normal temperature is around 101 degrees.

The Maine Coon Cat is a great big longhair. People love it. It would be dangerous to criticize it, and what is there to criticize?

They're considered the indigenous American cat; since America's history is so brief, a hundred years makes an indigene. The notion of their part-raccoon heritage is charming, and if such a cross were possible I'd be first in line for a kit; but alas, it isn't. The accepted theory is that they're the result of plain short-hairs, brought from Europe by settlers, mixed with Persians or Angoras brought by seafarers, perhaps a Captain Coon, in the 1800s. I can't quarrel with authority, but it seems odd that this doesn't happen anymore. Cross a Persian and a house cat and you get a fluffy house cat. You get Sidney, round-eyed, lazy house cat. The first official Maine Coon, Captain Jenks of the Horse Marines, surfaced in 1861, not giving the genes much time to change in response to the environment. Besides, why were they all outside in the environment, these sons and daughters of Persians and house cats?

A romantic but unofficial theory implicates the Norwegian Forest Cat, a similar creature domestic in Scandinavia for centuries, and just possibly left on our northern coast by

Vikings long before Columbus. British experts sniff, and say the Coon is a recent and artificial breed, while the Norsk Skaukatt is ancient, pure, and natural, and not an ancestor because its back legs are longer, but it seems clear they're jealous; no British cat has such panache.

Inspecting a generous sampling of both, and all unversed in anatomy as I am, I found them very hard to tell apart.

Along about the time of the Civil War and after it, Coon Cats grew in popularity, attracted national attention, and won ribbons in shows until the Persian invasion at the turn of the century, when people lost interest in the mere native. Because they faded from the show circuit, show people thought they had become extinct, but of course they were doing just fine back home.

In the late 1920s, the naturalist Henry Beston spent a year on Cape Cod, writing his classic book *The Outermost House.* "Twice during the winter," he says, "I saw a wildcat of domestic stock hunting along the edge of the marsh, and marked how savagery had completely altered the creature's gait, for it slunk along, belly close to the grass, like a panther. A large brown cat with long fur and an extraordinarily foolish face."

Leaving aside the naturalist who thinks domestic cats stalk their prey standing up straight and tall, and the scientific description of its face as "foolish," surely he saw a Maine Coon Cat rustling its breakfast on the Cape, not in the least extinct and, foolish or not, at least as capable and independent as Mr. Beston, who kept bumming rides into town to buy his groceries.

Maine cats make splendid instructive parents, and the kittens, who adore them and mature slowly, shouldn't leave home till they're twelve weeks old. They grow into considerable cats, weighing eighteen pounds and up, and rather clumsy on their big snowshoe feet, with brushy raccoon tails, loud purrs, merry dispositions and a grand self-possession. They like water, and that bushy coat is protected by a water-resistant oil for swimming; even when soaked, a Coon Cat is said to dry in fifteen minutes.

I went to a party in the suburbs. At exactly eleven o'clock in the evening a guest said, "There's someone at the door." Our host opened the door and stood staring blankly out into the empty darkness at eye level while an enormous cat stalked in around his feet. It marched across the room, ignoring the guests all reaching to pat it and crying "What a beautiful cat!", and stopped in front of George and Pat, and looked at them. It did not meow or rub against their ankles; it stood there and looked at them. They jumped up and made their apologies, found their coats and said goodnight and left, following the Coon Cat, who led them out looking neither to left nor right, for all the world like the father of errant teenagers come to fetch them home.

Fine fellows.

The Manx cat is not part rabbit, though the *Britannica* does hint mysteriously at a possible derivation from "another species." As far as we know, rabbits mate only with other rabbits, and are looked on by cats more as dinner than romance, and the notion is only slightly more probable than the story of how they arrived late at the Ark and Noah slammed the door on their tails. They seem to come from the Isle of Man in the Irish Sea, but since this is an insignificant area of only 221 square miles, various theories are put forth as to what larger place they arrived from. Some say Spain, swimming ashore from a shipwrecked galleon of the Armada. Some say China or Japan, because there's a tailless cat of long history called the Japanese Bobtail, considered very lucky when it turns up in three colors, though actually it may have been Korean to start with. The most recent investigations, however, conclude that it's genetically quite a different cat, and the Manx may come from Man after all; one source observes that there are tailless dogs on Man.

A single stubborn authority maintains that there is no Manx cat, and taillessness is simply a genetic freak that can turn up in any breed at any time.

Some Manx cats have no tail at all, just a dimple at the base of the spine, and some, called "stumpies," have part of a tail, and some have proper tails. My sister's Mehitabel, long-haired and of unknown origin, has half a tail; two of her daughters have real tails, and the third has a two-inch downward hook of a tail like a spit curl.

Among the Manx, only the quite tailless cat is eligible for showing. But breeders need to keep a few stumpies around for breeding, because there's a lethal factor in the missing tail; in the mating of tailless cats, the third generation will be weak and sickly and the fourth will be stillborn. There's something a bit skewed in the human encouragement of such a suicidal trait.

Manx cats have plushy undercoats and long hind legs like rabbits, and they swim well, as befits islanders.

Gray cats are nice. All gray cats, recognized or not, are nice; when they're recognized they're called blue cats. Each nation claims to have its own, and though to the untrained eye they look remarkably alike, each nation feels its own is best.

Malaysia has its blue jungle cat, and the light gray cat of Cyprus has black pads on its feet. Malta has its Maltese cats, and American gray cats with no exotic connections were once always referred to as Maltese, giving them status above their littermates to the human eye.

The Korat, native of Thailand, is silvery with green or amber eyes. For centuries it could not be sold, only presented as a gift to a deserving friend because of its great luckiness, signifying wealth and crops and happy marriages.

The Russian Blue, in the more exalted version, came straight from the Imperial Palace; more prosaically, it came to England on cargo boats trading with Archangel in the far north, on the White Sea, a charming place for a cat to come from. They have dense, double-layered fur suitable for such northern cats, and graceful, delicate, long-boned bodies with long tails and big pointy ears. Their eyes are green.

Saha, in Colette's *The Cat*, was a Russian Blue, exquisite, sensitive, and adoring, whose master had to choose between her and his bride, and chose her.

Colette's own last cat was a Chartreux. The Chartreux is a French gray, and a country sort of cat, good-natured and simple, Méry says, solid and stocky and round-faced, with short legs and woolly fur and great enthusiasm for mousing. It's been around since the Middle Ages, and is said to have come from southern Africa with Carthusian monks who named it for their first monastery, La Grande Chartreuse.

The British Blue is a British citizen type, neat and sturdy-looking, with orange, yellow, or copper eyes. Some English experts think it's the same as the Chartreux, a notion patriotically ridiculed by the French. And some writers refer to both the British and the Russian as Icelandic cats.

Georges I, II, and III were all gray; Flanagan is gray; Al and Leila and their kittens are gray. Gray alley cats, American cats, melting-pot cats. Not blue, because born at random to cats of great ordinariness working plebeian breeding ranges: gray. Gray with a plushy density of fur, all the same length like sheared beaver. Gray with silvery edgings and highlights about the paws, the ears, the twinkling testicles. Gray with eyes as yellow as suns. Loyal. Cheerful. Enormously *likable* cats, cats for the daily living, the long haul; cats as sound and friendly as a loaf of good bread. Solid cats, but with a touch of delicacy as they come toward you across the morning grass, putting one foot tidily in front of the other like Siamese, tail high, happy to be there.

Geneticists would scoff, and say there is no gray cat, only a genetically diluted manifestation of black, but this isn't true. Grays are good for you. They make you feel better about life.

They're easy to love. Teddy Roosevelt's gray cat Slippers was always allowed at important diplomatic dinners, and the sixteenth-century poet du Bellay wrote in anguished mourning:

My heart is almost breaking in me
When I speak or when I write
For Belaud my small gray cat.

The Sidneys of the world, the random patches of black
and white, represent an interesting genetic battle in which
the white moves in an orderly progression. First the locket
under the chin, perhaps a bikini-pants crescent, then the bib,
then the white toes. The bib spreads down along the stomach and the toes creep up into stockings. Fingers of white
extend up the sides, broadening into peninsulas. It always
moves up from below; we never see a cat white on top and
black or gray or striped below. A cat in the next block to
me represents a late stage, white all over but for four or
five roundish black spots along the spine, more doggish
than cattish. And in a pet shop I saw the very last stand, a
white cat with a single brush-stroke of black on the top of
the head, between the ears; in the genetic chess game of
black against white, white has won.

Black-and-whites come in some pleasant patterns, like
Sidney's big clear butterfly over the head, and in some clut-
tered and unappealing ones, and the cats themselves are
various. In Judy's colony they form an astonishing majority,
their arrivals all quite unrelated, and their only common
trait is that they either love their home, or are inordinately
fond of food, or dislike adventure: all day long the cats of
other colors are invisibly off about their catly business in
woods and fields, and all day long there are six black-and-
whites disposed about the lawn where the feeding dishes
are, not communing with each other, each at least eight feet
from the next, but there. At dinnertime they will not need
to be called. Sidney too is a trencherman, never called for
dinner or before an approaching storm; he was already
home.

They're comfortable cats, the black-and-whites, and will
never run up the grocery bill by demanding designer food.
Mr. Eliot's amiable uncomplicated Jellicle cats are good ex-
amples.

* * *

So many blue-eyed white cats are deaf that an impressive weight of authority holds that all blue-eyed white cats are deaf, even that white kittens born blue-eyed whose eye color changes later stay deaf for as long as their eyes stay blue, miraculously developing hearing only after the color turns.

Barney is a blue-eyed white cat.

Barney can hear a cat chow drop three rooms away. Barney can hear the difference between milk and water being poured into a bowl.

He can hear his name whispered a block away. He can hear paint drying, grass growing, hair turning gray, time passing. He can hear words that have never been spoken and songs that no one else will ever hear.

He can hear me thinking about him.

I hope that clears up the matter.

Striped cats are basic. Stripes are so essentially cat that they're the bane of breeders, and come creeping forward out of the buried generations to flower in shadowy bands down the legs of cats that aren't supposed to have stripes. Stripes are the irresistible jungle that keeps on whispering in the well-bred ear.

Striped cats are satisfying to look at, with their elaborate, inscrutable details, the lavishment of necklaces and bracelets, the *M* for Mau inscribed on the forehead, and the infinitely pleasing shades of cream and tawny around the eyes, the nose, and the whisker pads with their dark freckles marking the base of each hair. Striped cats are household hieroglyphics, undeciphered messages washing their paws after dinner and waiting to be read. Is it our fault or theirs, or the strange language they're written in, that no one seems to have a deep personal relationship with a striped cat? The experts, agreeing for once, say that the striper is closest to the wild; several say that of all the colors of cat this is the best able to survive on its own, and that it's noticeably more independent and predatory than its siblings, and makes the best mouser. Is it true? It sounds about as scientific as that blondes have more fun. Could it be that we believe it ourselves, and treat the striper differently, more respectfully but less intimately, because this is serious cat here, not an extra child to be cuddled but the Cat by its Wild Lone, and the cat reacts aloofly? Or did it start out a bit more distant, a bit less cheery and loving, than its solid-color littermates? All I know is that none of the striped cats in my life have ever been intimates, just respected associates.

Not that they're unfriendly. There's a photograph of the older Ernest Hemingway sharing his dinner and apparently conversing with a striped cat on his table; it's just that it was probably Hemingway and not the cat who started the conversation, or else the cat was merely listening, or pretending to listen.

As to whether they survive better on their own, proving this would involve getting a number of cats of the same age and different colors and dropping them off in the woods, and coming back some months later and rounding up the survivors and weighing them. It sounds impractical.

They are very wonderful to look at, though. The sheer luxury of their design and shadings put all human attempts at personal decoration to shame. And even considered as the humble necessary mouser of the millennia, the unassimilated cat of barn and kitchen and cellar and granary, is that an unworthy calling? The striped cat is first of all a *cat*.

I'm looking at a photograph I took of two cats that I met, if "met" isn't too strong a word, in an isolated village on the Pacific coast of México. They were a mated pair and they lived around a beachside restaurant specializing in fish; the restaurant was open to the world on all four sides, so they came and went as they pleased. People fed them from the tables, though they never asked for food in any way we know as asking. They would sit near a table, looking at nothing and no one, gazing indifferently into space, until a piece of fish was dropped at their feet; they ate it without acknowledgment as if it had fallen from the sky.

Whose cats are those? I asked. A shrug and a laugh. They were no one's cats. They were their own cats. They lived there, that was all.

To the best of my limited knowledge, they were Egyptian Gloved Cats, the image of the cat in the temple I'd seen on television. Broken stripes of black on gray, tawny cheeks and ears, barred legs and tail, white toes. Long cats, with long, long tails that had a curiously massive and imposing shape, like a cheetah's, narrowing as it joined the body, with broad assertive bands.

They were in splendid shape, elegant and strong. What were they doing here, these North Africans, half a world away in this scruffy, mountainous, appallingly poor stretch of western Mexico, where occasionally in the night bigger cats could be heard coughing in the hills? A pet cat here, if anyone could have imagined such a thing, would have starved along with its people.

When I approached and spoke to them, their indifference rebuked me. They didn't respond, and they didn't run away; they ignored me so utterly I felt rather drafty, as if abruptly disembodied, mixed with air. This is unsettling to humans. We're used to animals who either greet us or avoid us, or in some cases attack us, not animals for whom we simply don't exist. I felt diminished and a bit embarrassed, as if I had slapped the back of a stranger in a crowd.

This is how it was, then? Back in the beginning, with the first of people's cats? The only animal that showed us no fear, no hostility, and no acquiescence, that simply came to eat our fish and stare past us into space? No wonder we were fascinated. No wonder we searched out the hidden kittens and cuddled them, trying to coax some acknowledgment from those remote yellow eyes—if not thanks for the fish, then at least some hint that we were there, and seen.

We succeeded. Now we have only to ask in order to have one of our own, in our house, blinking affectionately at us and purring with pleasure in our company.

Traveling by various means, sailing with Phoenicians, jumping ship in strange ports, coming west with returning Crusaders, strolling across national borders in Southeast Asian jungles and Himalayan passes and East African deserts, traded for bananas or silk or amber, mating with the locals and moving on, cats cover the earth and spring up in such infinite variety it's a wonder any of us can be content with just two or three when there are so many others waiting to be known; a cornucopia of cats.

9

Show Business

The hall is arranged with rows of cages across its middle, seven judging rings along the sides, and things for sale at the ends. In the aisles between the cages exhibitors have set up housekeeping on folding tables and chairs and boxes and fallen to eating, napping, reading magazines, and playing cards, like a band of travelers in an airport waiting out a storm. It's hard to push past them, hard to see into the cages to the cats. But of course that's not the purpose of the thing; no one cares whether I see cats or not. These owners and breeders are dressed in a motley assortment of garments, as if there'd been a fire in the hotel, or all their luggage had gone astray. At dog and horse shows the people seem as much on view as the animals and size up each other's tweeds with covert glances, but these cat people give off a thorny intransigence and have scarcely bothered to comb their hair. After all, this isn't the big one. Madison Square Garden has already come and gone, leaving all hands with tales of its blizzard, and airports and highways closed; perhaps they dressed for that one, and have made their effort for the season.

This is only the second cat show of my life, and all I remember of the first one is that I took my impulsive little sister and she spent three weeks' salary on a rather self-

153

centered Persian kitten named Mokey, leaving me with the impression that they were dangerous events to attend, and of dubious purpose. Watching hunting dogs at field trials or horses racing, horses cutting cattle, or horses in the Handy Hunter Over Fences or the Knockdown and Out, it's nice to see what animals can do. They seem to like it too, and why not? It's satisfying to do things well, whether or not they appreciate the competitive point of view and the ribbons afterward. But cats are shown only for their looks, and how their looks conform to standards inexplicable to the cat or even the uninitiated human. The catliness of them is not at issue; they might as well be framed and hung on the wall.

Here I am, though. Stepping warily. Prepared to sneer.

The program says the exhibitors will be happy to explain and discuss their cats with me, but the program is wrong. Even people with signs saying "Kittens for Sale" are laconic and suspicious and go on laying out a round of solitaire. Maybe they were up too late last night, or got up too early to polish fur and backcomb tails. They barely chat among themselves, and no one greets another with cries of recognition; this is not a social occasion. They sit, blocking the view, in front of their cages, each of which has a sign saying "I'm Friendly But My Owner Bites," or "Touch Not the Cat," or "Don't Touch Me Even if I Ask," or "Your Kind Affection Could Result in Infection." Some cages are fronted with plastic wrap. I feel a bit leprous, my hands aswarm with invisible poisons.

Most of the cats are sensibly asleep.

One of the cages in the first row contains a patterned dollhouse rug on the floor, an elaborate standing lamp, and a four-poster bed with chintz bolsters and matching ruffled coverlet on which a Persian kitten is asleep. It's a pretty kitten in one of those pale Persian designs I can't keep straight, Cameo maybe, and doesn't seem at all affronted by life in a dollhouse. Other cages are fitted with curtains for withdrawing behind, or triangular ledges in the corners for lolling on, and one cat has retired into a drawstring bag and left only an ear showing. Ribbons, I suppose from earlier shows, hang across the wire like medals on a military chest: Second Best in Division, Best in Class, Fifth Best Kitten.

Many people have invested in pipe-cleaner tarantulas to hang from the ceilings of the cages, and several cats have already hooked them down to chew on.

A number of cats are sleeping in their litter boxes, paws decorously curled under chests.

Later a prize will be awarded for the best-decorated cage. A stand at the end is selling cage decorations.

The stands are doing a brisk business in sacks of scientific cat food, stuffed plush cats, coat conditioners, silvery cat bracelets and pendants and cat-shaped plastic earrings, mountains of pins and T-shirts and bumper stickers and mugs and decals and dish towels saying "I (heart) My Cat," ". . . My Burmese," ". . . My Manx," and so on, carpeted posts and platforms called Custom Cat Houses, kitty candies, collars, books, toys, toys, toys. A genial girl has set up a stand featuring home-grown catnip and toys thereof; already she's sold out of the pots of growing catnip. I buy a plastic bag of the straight stuff, to be assured later at home that it is indeed the real thing.

An official-looking woman strides by with a blue-point Siamese on her shoulders, an incongruous Siamese of the old-timey, chunky, round-faced type; I try to speak to it, but the woman hurries on.

The standard of manners among the cats is high. No one yowls, no one rips its cage apart, no one seems angry or nervous, and only one of a pair of Burmese kittens is frightened to see me and tries to hide behind his sister. The rest are old-timers. All but the Household Pets are unneutered, but no cat seems interested in its neighbors or the cats passing to and from the judging rings.

People are eating from paper plates what looks like cat food; in their cages cats are not eating what looks like the same stuff.

I come to a pair of young Singapuras and stop to stare. I've never seen one before, and they give the whole hall a momentary zoolike feel. They have slick lion-blond fur, ticked like an Aby's, and cross-looking dark lines running down beside their noses like cheetahs. Natives of Singapore. Small but dangerous-looking; something you'd bring home as an orphan from the jungle only to have it turn savage later and eat your left arm. They're asleep, but they sleep alertly. If I woke up to find one of these curled on the pillow beside me, I expect I'd scream.

Shorthair kittens are being judged in ring 3, a ring being a stainless steel table in front of a bank of cages. The judge is holding up a white Oriental Shorthair by each end, like a length of ribbon, and discussing it quietly to herself; I think she says she'd like to see it lose a quarter of a pound. How? From where? Cut off one of its enormous ears? There's no cat there to reduce; it's narrow as a newt, an albino snake with albino bats for its ears. It's hardly wider than its own tail; where does it put its dinner? Every mouthful must leave a lump. Its head is shaped like a log-splitting wedge; its legs are thin as pencils. I try to imagine it taking its place in the semicircle of barn cats around old Mrs. Reid, who was Finnish and milked by hand, and catching its squirt of milk when its turn came. Try to imagine it catching a mouse, or even a spider.

The judge puts it back in its cage next to a black sample of the same thing, the insides of whose ears are pure white, like a black satin smoking jacket lined with white silk. All these cats are like something else besides cats, exaggerated beyond cathood into artifact.

In the next ring a judge returns two Persians to their cages, held on high in each hand like a giant's orange fur mittens.

My judge picks up a plumey feather and walks along the cages waving it at the bars. Some jump for it, gaining points, I suppose; others merely stare and look offended. The kitten in the last cage screams like a rusty gate: a Siamese. The only Siamese in the class. She continues to yowl after the judge moves on, as if suddenly fed up with the proceedings, reminded by the feather maybe that there are better things to do.

Once focused on her, my eyes don't want to leave, and I stand there gaping and tracing over her shapes, drawn in brown-black ink on cream-colored paper; the precise coil of her thin, dark tail against her creamy hip could not be improved by all the calligraphers in Japan. As she sits there shouting at no one, her furious little profile is a bone-and-fur reconstruction of what every unborn creature must hope to look like, sooner even than a swan or a luna moth. Probably she was a saint in some earlier round of things, as the Birman cats are said to embody the souls of dead priests, and the purity of her first life, dedicated to constant contemplation of some single perfect truth, is reborn in these lines and colors. There's nothing luxurious about her, nothing lavish or extra; she's an ink drawing, not a painting, and I lace my hands behind my back not to accidentally touch and smudge it. If she were mine, I'd probably forget to feed her, or feed her on drops of honey like a hummingbird. Herb tea in a painted porcelain cup.

It dawns on me that one of the two men standing beside me owns her. I slide him a sideways glance: an ordinary mortal sort of man. His companion is saying, "I remember you said you were pleased with her refinement."

"Refinement"? Well, yes, if that's the best word we can find. "Refined," as in gold.

The two men have their catalogs folded back and make marks in them, apparently understanding something from their pages. I open my own copy. To me it's an Arabic train schedule, a Coptic stock-market report. "JB MC PM BM, AB AB AB AB. BR/OW. (NE) 0.11. SGC TYPHA NITE SPRITE." Where am I? I search for the same page they have. All right, if this is really the page, and this is the only SP kitten, then her name is Soroko Forever Amber. Preposterous, there's nothing amber about her; if he must name cats from his bookcase, why not Soroko The Jungle Book? Soroko Anna Karenina? The man's unworthy. The man, if I have the right page and the right cat, is listed as a doctor.

Not even a Buddhist priest. And why isn't she looking at him? She shouts, but she's glaring off somewhere to the left.

I don't really want his cat, though; it isn't because of her that I've left my checkbook safely at home. There's no place to put her where I live. Be she ever so adaptable, there is no corner in my house, no chair, no windowsill, that she wouldn't disgrace by her presence; nothing I own would be a suitable place for Soroko Forever Amber to sit. And what of the doctor? He's listed as BR/OW, which must mean breeder/owner, which must mean he has a houseful of these, or a catteryful; does he keep them in cages, rows of them in patient captivity, with the thin white flames of their holiness waiting for rebirth or liberation to nirvana?

He seems discontented. Listening, I learn that if the show had been just one day later she would have been eight months old and eligible to show as an adult. This kitten class counts for nothing, doesn't accumulate the right kind of points; it's practice only, a waste of his time. He scowls and ruffles the pages of his catalog, his karma roiled and seething.

The judge hangs ribbons from the cages, the doctor goes to get his cat, and I turn away, remembering only later that I hadn't noticed if she won anything. I think one of the Chartreux kittens beat her, handsome chubby fellows. It doesn't seem to matter.

Needing solid earth, I go to visit the Household Pets, and speak to them in normal, irreverent tones. There are fewer vigilant owners on guard here, so they're easier to see. Unburdened by family standards to uphold, they look well fed, these normal cats, and unremarkable, and I'm secretly pleased that none is as stylish as my little black Spider, and none of the black-and-whites has Sidney's sweet nose and outlined eyes, or his whimsical markings. A spark of competitiveness darts through me; it must be in the air here: I should have brought Spider. Spider would win. I leaf through a booklet they've given me to the piece on Household Pets. They're judged, it says, giving 25 points for their

looks, 15 for personality, and 60 for "condition." A health
contest, then. That must be hard to gauge; it's easy to see
how sick a sick cat is, but how do you measure its health-
iness on, say, a scale of one to ten? Sickness is relative;
health, unless they've planned a rope climb and some foot-
races to assess it, is health. I won't bring Spider; this is pa-
tronizing, a contest for schoolchildren, complete with
lecture on nutrition afterward. I can see the point, in a way,
of judging how good an Aby an Aby is, how like the perfect Aby, but there's no way to judge the goodness of a
Household Pet; that's a private matter between pet and person.

The woman with the blue point on her shoulder hurries
past again, cat swaying, and I realize to my chagrin that
this isn't a hefty old-time Siamese at all, but a Tonkinese,
a new Burmese-Siamese blend. After all the years of narrowing and shrinking the Siamese and sharpening its angles, people must have been nostalgic for the old ones, and
turned them backward with Wong Mau's blood into meatier
cats again, with softer fur and gentler faces.

I don't belong here; I'm out of my depth; I don't even
recognize half what I'm looking at.

I look for and don't find the highly publicized California
Spangled Cat, something new that's been rather a celebrity
and appeared on television. Somebody dedicated almost beyond the point of sanity took eleven generations to produce
it, working with a Siamese, Silver Tabby, Manx, Abyssinian, Cat of the Nile, Brown Tabby, Malayan Tropical
Housecat, and a Spotted Silver Longhair: a veritable cat
stew. It has spots. It was featured in the Neiman-Marcus
Christmas catalog as "a leopard for your living room" and
sold for fourteen hundred dollars; they had dozens more orders than kittens, and the waiting list is years long. In spite
of its price it hasn't been recognized as a breed yet, so it
gets to stay home in the living room instead of traveling
around in a box.

Someone has taken a Scottish Fold from its cage for a
quick touch-up, and I've never seen one of these before

either. The fancy-cat world moves too fast for me. They're one of the genetic accidents, descended from a farm cat named Susie born in 1961 in Perthshire with her ears folded down. This struck the neighbors as interesting, and they put her into the kitten business. Breeding from only a single, accidental cat, they ran into problems and some of the Folds were born with skeletal deformities and some were born deaf, but the breeders, so fiercely do we lust for peculiar cats, persevered, and they're well established now, with fifty or more catteries doing business in the United States. They're said to be gentle and playful cats who like to sleep on their backs and to sit around on their haunches with their tails stuck out behind like beavers.

Now I hear we're about to have something similar of our own, the American Curl, whose ears bend inward as if it were standing in a private eddy of wind.

This Fold submits to a small plastic blade that scoops and peaks up the fur on its nose to a jaunty ridge, visible at close quarters and lasting only until the first paw swipe. The folded ears alter its expression so much that I can't tell how it feels or what it's thinking. What do other cats make of it? It looks a little like an owl and a little like a Beatrix Potter cat wearing a bonnet; Tom Kitten's mother, maybe.

One problem, I understand, is that the female's ears straighten out when she goes into heat, and may or may not fold up again afterward. While I'd love to be around at the onset of estrus to watch the ears unfurl with longing, it still seems less cat than conversation piece, and I always worry that there may be a God somewhere who doesn't like us fooling around with His cat like this.

At least it wears fur, though, fur like a cat. This show has a generous share of curly Rexes and wrinkled, naked, suede Sphynxes; it even turns out that there are two kinds of Rex, Cornish and Devon. "Elfin" is the word the booklet uses, and perhaps elves are what they look like, elves from outer space. I study them with quick glances and look away again as my mother told me to: "Don't stare, darling, it's rude." They're tiny cats with ears bigger than their heads and bulging out sideways like loaded saddlebags. How did we make them look like this in such a short time, starting from a farm in Cornwall in 1950 and an accidentally curly kitten named Kallibunker? And, of course, why? From the corner of my eye I stare at a cat intended to be black and white but actually, thanks to our tireless efforts, black and pink; the rows of short, soft, poodley curls are so sparse that pink skin shows through. Its face is a tiny dog's face under the absurd ears; we're ambivalent about ears, apparently, so that Persians and Folds are admired for having almost none, while these poor creatures must need guy ropes on a windy day. Its whiskers are gnarled stubs, as if a wicked child had singed them with a match.

Embarrassed for it, I go off to watch the judging of Norwegian Forest Cats. Now, these are cats, real cats, these Norsk Skaukatts, an honest armful of cat with honest whiskers and long, solid fur. For some reason we humans were pleased with them just as they were, and no effort has been made to make them twice as much like themselves. I check my pocketbook to make sure I have indeed left my checkbook at home.

There's one in particular, a female (even I can see that some of the numbers are on pink cards and some on blue) whose mix of cream and dark fur, whatever it's called, is pleasing to look at and whose charm and cheerfulness flow from her cage. Behind the judge's back she has hooked a prize ribbon from outside her cage and brought it inside with a delicate curled paw, and pats it around the floor and chews on its string. When the judge takes it away and fastens it up more firmly, she turns her attention to the male in the next cage, reaching her paws out to play with him, standing up to show us the waterfall of fur down her stomach. A feminine cat, the creamy ruff and flowing bib showing off her sweet face like a hat on a pretty girl, and she likes the young man next door. I will have them both, then, and have kittens.

The checkbook is safely home on the bureau.

The judge gives the feather test; only this judge uses an orange ball on a bouncy wire, and one cat cringes and hisses at it. My cat reaches out for it with both arms to the shoulder through the bars. A happy cat. I try to look her up in the catalog, but I can't find my way through the pages.

The judge passes out ribbons, but I don't know what they mean. Cat shows are not a spectator sport. Any fool at a horse show can see Number 27 refuse the In-and-Out, or hear the bonk when a hock clips the top bar, but in this place you have to belong to know what's going on. Or, I suppose, to care.

I pick my way back through the card tables, down the row of Rexes. The black-and-pink has been taken from its cage by its owner, a motherly-looking woman in a low-cut blouse seated on a folding chair. I smile nervously down at it. I'm told they feel warm to the touch, like puppies, because of the short fur. I try not to notice its whiskers.

As I pass, it worms its way up the woman's front and buries its face in her neck, nuzzling and licking, and begins to purr. I stop to listen; yes, it's purring. *Purring? That?* I'm as shaken as if a frog had said "meow." Distorted, monstrous, warped by human meddling till God Himself wouldn't know it as a cat, it thrusts its head against its human's neck and purrs as if it had a right to purr. It's a *cat.* I suppose it must eat its dinner and wash its paws, sprawl on the rug in the sunshine, all those things, as if it didn't know or humbly accepted what we've done to it. All our long, expensive efforts to turn cat into not-cat have been in vain; strong as wire, catness still runs humming through the generations of increasingly uncatlike cats, and just like Kallibunker's mother on her Cornish farm, this thing can purr. Leave it alone for a few generations and it would cure its own monstrosity, flesh out, grow fur, have real ears and whiskers. Persians that snuffle like bulldogs would grow their noses back; Siamese that look like strings would broaden, and catch mice.

The cat triumphant. Cats 10; people 0.

Satisfied, I get my coat and leave.

10

Medical Matters

Cats feel pretty good most of the time. They rarely indulge in the ailments so popular on television: the common cold, flu, headaches, insomnia, sinus pain, indigestion, lower back pain, hangovers, coffee nerves, sore throats, and sunburn. On any given day they probably feel better than we do. They live the way we should, and while they may eat an occasional button or length of thread, they never go out and buy junk food full of salt, fats, and sugar, and they don't need exercise clubs to keep the muscles taut; an occasional dash up the curtains and a little stretching does it.

Their talent for sleeping anywhere and any time is enviable. Their capacity for contentment keeps the heart and nerves and gastric juices in the pink. If they've eaten unwisely, and even sometimes when they haven't, they vomit swiftly and easily. They do not stress their systems with office politics, nuclear war, the stock market, or whether their children are using drugs, but live contained in the savored moment, an example to us all. And the lucky cats of responsible people have the advantage of dizzying recent progress in feline veterinary medicine.

It's as well they don't get sick often, because a sick cat is a discouraging creature to nurse. We go to the grocery store and buy a lamb chop, get down the heating pad and the cashmere shawl, sit beside it, and speak gently; it turns its head aside. A cat friend licks its head and ears and curls up next to it; it turns its head aside. Struggles to its feet and staggers off the heating pad, out from under the shawl, steps over the bits of lightly broiled lamb chop and crouches on the cold bare floor with eyes averted: it will not take comfort. Cats can sicken with terrifying suddenness, and in this as in other things they do not persevere; like the American Indian of cherished legend they compose themselves for death. Love and kindness cease to matter, and they avoid looking us in the eye, lest we learn what they have in mind.

A cat in extremis will manage to get to the front door, even if it has never been outside, and scratch at it, begging permission to go away and be alone with dying. Go out and meet it halfway.

All the more urgency for professional medical care, with cats; for doctors to grab the departing cat by the scruff of the neck, so to speak, overrule its decision, and snatch it back to us.

Sometimes. Not always, of course. Not forever.

Sidney is sick. Sidney, who has never been sick for a moment in his seventeen years, has one of the swift and sudden cancers of feline leukemia virus. One day he was playing with the kitten and wolfing down his dinner, and the next day he sat hunched between his elbows looking at the floor. The cancer can be treated to a certain extent, but only until the kidneys go.

The kidneys go.

Two Siamese cats, kindly young Morgan and cross old Corvo, sit one on each side of him and lick him tirelessly. His white patches have never been so clean.

You'll know, the vet says; his back legs will give out.

His back legs give out. Flopping and staggering, he makes his way to the front door and asks permission to leave.

Morgan, Corvo, and my daughter sit up with him all night. He sighs, he moves from one position to another, uncomfortable everywhere. He goes back to the door and hooks a paw under it. Morning comes. Wrapped in a bright red towel, he makes his last trip to the vet.

It's a decision often described as harrowing, but not now, not here. It's almost a joy, and a fine thing we have in our hands here for our cats, to shorten the hard journey. Lift them over the last bad mile.

We can't do this for people we love, but we can do it for our cats and rejoice. We can't give our children a good life, either; all we can do is start them on their way and hope; we can give our cats a good life. We cry, of course, everyone cries, but we keep saying to each other, Didn't he have a grand time of it, though? Didn't we spoil him, the old slob? He was always petted and babied, even the other cats babied him, in all his life he never once washed his own face. He was an uncomplicated cat, and easily content. He loved to eat and to sit in the sun. He had a fine time.

The saddest note is young Morgan, who searches the house for days, upstairs and down, wearing herself to a rag and pausing only to stand in front of me and shout angrily into my face; she seems to think I have lost him, and forgotten about him. All she knows is that he was sick and she was taking care of him, and now he's nowhere to be found; perhaps in the basement, weak and forgotten behind some boxes? Perhaps up on the third floor accidentally closed in a closet? How can I sit there, and not join her in looking? She is furious with me and will not be touched.

I hope someday there will be a pill for home use, and that last frightening trip not be necessary, and the cats and people gather around the familiar couch to say good-bye, and the cats know what became of a friend.

After a week or so she stops looking. Life goes on.

The first rule of cat ownership is to protect ourselves from guilt. "Well, we did everything possible ..." is sad enough to have to say, but it doesn't sting like "If only we'd ..."

When things end badly, it helps to know we had the world's best vet. It's important to be sure. Most of them are conscientious, but some are more skillful surgeons, and better informed. Some are principally interested in dogs and don't make the steady effort to keep up with fast-breaking developments in cat treatment. A cheerful, confident, friendly bedside manner with the human client is no indication of anything, any more than it is with car salesmen. Not being doctors ourselves, the best we can do is ask around. Ask as many people as we can think of, all the cat owners we meet, breeders, shelters, local cat clubs, everyone. Bring the subject up at the office and at parties. People who are pleased with their vet are more than anxious to tell us about it; it's a kind of one-upmanship: "Oh, you don't go to *him*? You have to go to *my* vet, mine's the best." Tabulate the answers. Consider the circumstances. If we hear that Dr. A is a murderer, ask what happened. Did he overdose the cat, miss an easy diagnosis, leave a pair of dirty socks in the incision? Or did his patient die of lymphosarcoma at the age of twenty-three? It's a delicate matter, losing your cat, and everyone feels that more should have been done, up to and including miracles. On the other hand, if several otherwise sane people tell us Dr. A killed their cats, we'd better check Dr. B.

There's an undeniable charm about holistic medicine and the idea of curing disease with old-fashioned, gentle, sweet-smelling teas and baths of herbs and flowers and wholesome natural things like yeast and garlic. Lots of these naturopathic remedies, inspected under controlled conditions, turn out to be beneficial. Mildly beneficial. The problem can lie in the mildness, and a vet wholly dedicated to this kind of care may go on treating a cat with vitamin C, rosemary, and pennyroyal long after strong intervention with cold heartless antibiotics is called for. Gentle is good sometimes, and sometimes modern, fierce, unnatural, invasive, sudden, surgical or chemical attacks will save the small life; an abstract conviction is worth only so much. Probably, from the cat's point of view, very little; cats aren't given to convictions. Those of us personally committed to natural medicine should at least look for a vet who's not too proud to admit its limitations, and one who is indeed a VMD and not just a kindred spirit with a book about herbs.

All praise to preventive vaccines. There was a time when sensible persons held back a bit before taking a young cat to their hearts, because it was almost as likely to die as not. Now our standard essential package protects against enteritis, rhinotracheitis, and calici virus, making it far safer to get fond of a kitten. (If we get a kitten billed as having "had his shots," it's best to find out exactly what shots; it was probably just early temporary protection, needing reinforcement.) A cat who goes outdoors needs a rabies shot, required by law in many states, with boosters every one to three years as recommended by our vet or insisted on by our state.

The best news in recent years is the Leukocell vaccine, available since 1985, that protects against the number-one killer, feline leukemia virus, known in cat circles as FeLV; I don't know how they pronounce it.

The leukemia virus destroys the cat's immune system, leaving it open to cancers, most commonly lymphosarcoma, respiratory diseases, feline infectious peritonitus, and thymic atrophy. It's contagious from cat to cat, though not from cat to person, and the virus is passed saliva from licks or bites. It can infect unborn kittens through the placenta, and born kittens through the milk. The commonest age of onset is around two or three years, and the common signs are malaise, anorexia, weight loss, fever, lethargy, and enlargement of the lymph glands.

When a cat's been exposed, various things can happen. It may not be infected at all. Or it may get infected but neutralize the virus somehow, and wind up not only healthy but resistant to future infections. Or it may be infected but not sick, and carry the virus in latent form. Or, finally, it may get infected and develop one of the related diseases, with a death rate around eighty percent. It can take a while to show up; the official word is from a few weeks to a few months, but Sidney hadn't seen a cat outside the family for eight months, and all the other cats tested negative.

The tests aren't absolutely accurate. A negative answer means only that the cat wasn't carrying the virus at the time the blood sample was taken, and it may even have been in the earliest stages of infection. It's a good idea to do a second test later. Positive answers don't show whether it has or may get one of the related diseases, but even if it doesn't, it will shed the virus and shouldn't hang around with other cats until they've been inoculated.

Negative cats who may have been exposed should have the series of three Leukocell vaccinations. It's a nuisance, but it beats the possible alternatives.

More good news: in 1987, cats with the killer heart disease called dilated cardiomyopathy, curable only by heart transplant, were found to have inadequate amounts of an essential nutrient called taurine in their bloodstreams. Its addition to their diets cured the condition, which had killed tens of thousands of cats a year in the United States.

Pet food makers were alerted, and moved quickly to add taurine supplements to products that tested deficient in it. (This breakthrough may eventually prove to be good news to humans with congestive heart failure, if a correlation can be found.)

On the bad-news side stands hyperthyroidism. The first cases of this surfaced in 1980, so the older books don't mention it, but it's showing up more and more frequently among the senior cats.

The early signs can even look cheering to the cat's people. When a torpid, overweight old cat begins to perk up and spring around the house ruffling the rugs, eats more enthusiastically and yet slims down, it looks like a whole new lease on life, but it might be hyperthyroidism. It's caused by a thyroid adenoma, an enlargement of the thyroid gland that makes it secrete too much thyroid hormone. This sends the cat's metabolism into the racing mode. Fat and muscle tissue are consumed, high blood pressure can lead to heart and kidney failure, and circulating immune complexes get trapped in the kidneys and damage them further. Things to look for in the cat over seven or eight are weight loss, increased appetite, hyperactivity, increased drinking and urination, heart murmur, vomiting shortly after eating, diarrhea or larger stools, and difficulty breathing. If you spot more than a couple of these, take him in for a blood test.

The best treatment, as of now, is what humans get, with radioactive iodine taken up by the tumor tissue and destroying it. But unfortunately, it's expensive and not widely available for cats. It's also possible to remove the abnormal gland or glands surgically, a fairly tricky procedure but the treatment of choice right now. There are also medications, propylthiouracil or tapazole, that control it to an extent but have some side effects. Dr. Susan McDonough, vet of final authority in these parts and a kind of feline Surgeon General, currently uses them only as a preparation for surgery.

Most recently, cases are beginning to crop up in more than one cat in a family, meaning that there may be some infectious agent involved, or a culprit in the environment. Dr. McDonough thinks it might hinge on diet, and hopes that thorough research on cat foods may pinpoint it.

In the meantime we have to cast a skeptical eye on the magically rejuvenated older cat.

Back to good news: nonsurgical hope for the cat with Feline Urinary Syndrome, familiarly known as FUS to vets and cystitis to the rest of us. It isn't cystitis; that's an inflammation of the urinary tract. With FUS, the urine forms crystals in the bladder or urethra that make urination painful and difficult or impossible. It happens only to males, and without quick treatment it can lead to uremic poisoning and death. The cat makes frequent sad trips to the litter box, and strains and cries, and produces little. Boy was a martyr to it before much could be done for it, and notified me of attacks by going to the bathroom and pulling down all the towels and sprinkling each with a few agonizing bloody drops. A vet with a catheter relieved the immediate problem, and then there were little red pills that may or may not have helped, and then it would happen again.

Some cats never get it, and some cats, on the same diet and leading the same life, do; they're called FUS cats by their vets, because once it's happened it's very likely to happen again. It's a sad problem. With an old or chronically ill cat you always have the option of ending his troubles, but what to do with a fine young friend in perfect health except for these spells of dreadful pain and danger?

Diet was always suspected as a factor. More than one doctor blamed the use of cereal in cat foods. Ash was considered a major villain, and pet food manufacturers made great news of their low ash content. We were told never to feed male cats fish. We were told never to feed FUS cats dry food. We were told to feed them anything but to salt it heavily, so they would drink more water and dilute the urine. Now, finally, they seem to have gotten it right, and put the finger on the acid/alkaline balance in the urine. Acidic urine won't let the crystals form; alkaline will, and happily it's no great matter to lower the urine pH to the desired 6.2 to 6.4.

At Dr. McDonough's Cat Hospital of Philadelphia, the cat arriving with his first FUS attack is given a quick urinary-tract acidifier plus ammonium chloride for long-range management, and put immediately on Prescription Diet c-d, from Hill's Pet Products, one of the delicately compounded designer cat foods available from vets and pet shops but not from supermarkets. As a preventive measure, the hospital recommends Science Diet Feline Maintenance, and both are just fine for the other members of the family. If the condition recurs, and Dr. McDonough believes it extremely unlikely if the people in charge of the can opener stick to the diet, the cat's second attack is followed by urinary bypass surgery.

The very thought will make the sympathetic human wince, but it's now a safe and standard operation that repositions and widens the opening of the urethra so that the crystals can slip easily through. Its only drawback is the slightly increased risk of urinary infections because of the wider opening, but at that the risk is no greater than females run to begin with.

Still, if the problem can be wiped out by controlled diet, it's madness to put a cat through surgery.

Dr. Shelley Blum at Blum Animal Hospital in Chicago does ongoing independent research on food for the FUS cat, and his list of canned food goes: Prescription Diet c-d and Science Diet Feline Maintenance, Friskies and Fancy Feast beef and liver, and 9 Lives country chicken and gravy, choice cuts and cheese, tuna and chicken, savory stew, and beef and egg.

A spokesman for the company that does research for Carnation products says their dry foods, Friskies, Chef's Blend, Fish Ahoy, and Bright Eyes, create a most acceptable 6.2 pH urine. Iams, a rapid riser in the special-foods world, makes a dry food with a low magnesium content that's becoming increasingly popular for FUS management. Purina, at this writing, feels the whole concept of urinary acidity is still too new for comment.

Dry food for the FUS cat was under a cloud for years, but Dr. McDonough suggests that this may be from the way it's fed. After eating, she says, an alkaline tide is automatically released and raises the cat's pH. Dry food is usually left out for whenever the cat feels peckish, and the frequent snacking keeps the alkalinity coming. Serve it as a meal, then take it away.

This seems like rather a lot on the subject of a few tiny crystals, but anyone who's been through it with a sufferer, even if the good news comes too late, rejoices in it.

On the subject of normal diet for normal cats, much is written, much of it contradictory. Books from Britain confuse the American reader with recipes; British cat food, if it exists, must be a disaster, and proper cat owners cook. Not that they agree with each other. Some feed only raw food, darkly hinting at the effects of cooking; pregnant females fed cooked food, for instance, have but few and sickly kittens, often stillborn. Their colleagues hotly maintain that raw food is virtually poisonous for cats, leaving us to imagine cats in less protective times grilling their mice over tiny outdoor barbecues. One says nothing but raw beef, the perfect food; another warns of the dire effects of pork; another says one-third of the meal should be such cooked vegetables as leeks, asparagus, lettuce, carrots, and endive. Cat-keeping in England is hard work. One writer's cat "makes a habit / Of eating nothing else but rabbit," prepared fresh daily. Another says the diet must be supplemented with boiled oatmeal and milk. Europeans pour their cats a lot of milk, while the American feeling is that it's bad for adult cats. The fact is, digesting milk is related to an enzyme that some cats lose when they grow up and some don't. If our particular cat doesn't get diarrhea from milk, there's nothing wrong with it.

Americans are blessed with a busy and competitive pet-food industry. To watch the television commercials you'd think they didn't have a brain in their heads, but in truth they're backed by professional research teams as much concerned with nutrition as with talking cats. American cat food is good stuff, at least the recognized brands; we're warned against generic cat food as lacking quality control and possibly containing whatever was cheap and handy at the moment.

The disciplinarians say it's sentimental to suppose our cats need or want variety in their meals, but Dr. McDonough recommends it; there may be things we haven't yet learned about nutrition, and it's safest to touch as many bases as possible. Besides, the single-food cat can be a problem. A cat fixated on tuna, for instance, may develop kidney troubles and have to give up tuna as too high in phosphorus, and then compound its problems by refusing to consider anything else. (A few years back, tuna cat food made feline news as the villain in steatitis, a particularly vicious inflammatory disease, but the addition of vitamin E has eliminated the problem, and the only steatitis victims the Cat Hospital sees now have been eating human tuna, without the supplement, a most mistaken kindness.)

Controversy rages over canned versus dry food, with a heavy weight of authority on the side of the dry, often with a noticeably puritanical ring to it. Those who favor strict rules and discipline for cats seem to insist on dry food as well, as if canned food were a wanton luxury, a dietary satin cushion guaranteed to produce whining, spoiled, demanding children. It isn't. However, chewing dry food is a kind of feline toothbrush, and may help prevent some dental problems. At this house, having no FUS cats, we have our saucers of dry food topped off with small amounts of our favorite canned stuffs for excitement; the topping is eaten at once and the crunchy part picked at later.

The "soft-moist" foods in their convenient packets are poorly regarded and often referred to as junk food. I looked up some of the ingredients once in a king-size dictionary and found that one of them is also used in embalming corpses; probably there's nothing wrong with eating it, but it isn't something you'd order from a menu if you had a choice.

Dr. McDonough offers no people food to cats at all, but most of us don't see the harm in sharing an occasional treat. Some cats get quite excited over it; Sidney, admirer of human customs, was delighted by scraps of this and that, but only at the table, where humans ate. Others will accept them only in their dishes, where cats eat. And still others glare, suspect poison, and scratch imaginary dirt over anything that isn't cat food. Those of us lazily given to canned or frozen human dinners will get a dismaying look of reproach if we offer to share; perhaps we'd be better off sharing theirs.

I've always felt an egg yolk, fork-beaten with a dash of milk, was a wholesome small luxury, but we should throw away the white.

The puritanical experts are also severe about overweight, and to be sure it's no better for him than for us to get fat, and a cat without enough to occupy his mind may get obsessed with meals and overeat just for something to do. But with a busy, healthy cat I don't see any sense in fussing around weighing him, and measuring out his tablespoon of breakfast. The fattest cat I ever knew, a neighborhood gent named Junior Reynoldson, was reputed to weigh thirty pounds, and died under a lilac bush at the age of twenty-four, having enjoyed an excellent life. Perhaps if he'd been severely dieted he would have lived to be thirty, or perhaps he would have lost interest in life and died young. It was his vocation, his calling, to be an enormous cat.

A cat that goes off its feed may be sickening with something, or there may be another problem, requiring thought on our part. Corvo, for instance, refused his food for several days and sat in the kitchen doorway watching the others eat. Before I rushed him to the vet it occurred to me that he wanted to be *fed* in the kitchen doorway, as a mark of distinction from other cats, a sign that, while the others, of whatever breed, feeding in a row under the table, were only cats, he was *Corvo*. It's a great nuisance stepping over his dish in the doorway now, but he eats well.

All books tell us to keep a bowl of clean, fresh water available and change it daily, and of course we should. I do, and sometimes, when there are no foul-smelling marigolds rotting in a handy vase, no muddy puddles, leaking faucets, damp bathtubs, or melting ice in a whiskey glass, and someone has put the toilet lid down, they are forced to drink some of it.

Cats eat grass. Nobody knows why. Some claim it's because they need it in their diets, and instruct us to keep a pot of it growing in the house in winter and for indoor cats. They don't explain what possible nutritive use it is if the cats are going to keep throwing it up on the rug the way they do, unchanged and only slightly marked by teeth, since cats are not cows. It's also been put forth that they eat the grass because they need to throw up; but how is it, then, when you open the door on a sunny May morning, that every cat in the house suddenly needs to throw up and runs out to eat grass?

Contrary advice claims that eating grass is bad for them and fills them with parasites and we should prevent it, an athletic job if we have several outdoors cats; we'll need to hire assistants. Nutritious or not, they can't stop themselves.

I've been told that when cats eat grass it's a sign of rain.

Perhaps that's it. They eat grass to tell us it's going to rain, and come to throw it up at our feet to make sure we noticed and will take our umbrellas.

Cats eat grass. There are always some mysteries left.

Whether or not they're eating grass, they do get uninvited guests from time to time. Roundworms are the commonest. They can arrive in kittens via their mother, or be passed on in the litter pan or just from the great outdoors. They produce flatulence, diarrhea, pot belly, retching, and vomiting; the worms themselves appear in the vomit, curled up into little spirals; hence, roundworms. Tapeworms are most commonly transmitted by fleabites, and advertise their presence with little white rice grains around the cat's anus. As usual, we're discouraged from using supermarket medicines for them without consulting our vet.

Ear mites pass easily from cat to cat, and strays come fully equipped with them even more often than with incipient kittens. They itch. I've seen a cat kick its ears to bloody shreds from a particularly bad mess of them; with a lighter infestation the host just sits around with its ears at half-mast and an inward expression on its face, scratching moodily from time to time. Mites prefer the short and furry ear to the naked, drafty caverns of the Siamese, and are said to be at their happiest in the lop-eared Scottish Fold. You can get drops for them from your vet, but it's best to let him do the initial scrape-out, since most of us are too timid, and rightly so, to be sufficiently savage and thorough.

Fleas are among the most successful inhabitants of the earth. If, as we're told, there will still be cockroaches around after the nuclear holocaust, the cockroaches will probably have fleas.

One cat book says, reproachfully, that the well-cared-for cat seldom "catches fleas," but I don't see why a bright flea wouldn't actually prefer a tender, plushy cared-for cat to a slat-sided, thin-coated stray. Surely the attention of fleas is a compliment?

Some cats have an allergic reaction to their bite and

some seem hardly to notice them, but all can get tapeworm from them. And in a suitably welcoming environment, a happily married pair of fleas can give us six thousand youngsters within a month.

Some years seem to favor them. One summer, in the country, the whole county had fleas. Even people with no resident livestock had them, and people with cats and dogs beggared themselves with collars and sprays and bombs, and still they came. Only Rachel and her two cats had no fleas. Rachel put brewers' yeast in their food. There wasn't a flea in the place; it was a refuge for the flea-bitten neighbors, and as we sat there scratching our ankles and brooding we noticed there were no screens in the windows and no flies in the house. Rachel planted tansy under the windows to keep out flies.

I don't know about the tansy, but scientific tests prove that brewers' yeast has very little effect on fleas. My private feeling is that it had something to do with the faith and personal goodness of Rachel herself, and if *I* relied on yeast and tansy the cats and I would be bare, bleached bones by morning.

Garlic doesn't help either, they say.

Once you've got fleas, there's no use just tackling the cat's, you've got to do the house. A recommended fogger is Siphotrol-Plus, with both instant and long-range action. Spray areas the fogger doesn't reach, and put some mothballs or a flea collar in the vacuum-cleaner bag and vacuum daily for a while, to catch the eggs before they hatch. For the cat, there are collars and tags, sprays and roll-ons, powders, shampoos, a whole arsenal. The collars are all right if the fleas aren't too many and the cat isn't sensitive to them; they give Barney raging sores. Get collars from the vet instead of the supermarket. The sprays have the drawback of hissing like a hostile cat; the new Supra-Quick roll-on rolls on quietly, and it's safe for kittens too. A cat with battalions of fleas or a severe allergy to them should have a medicated shampoo; it takes the flea allergens away as well as the fleas, and leaves a repellent residue.

We all have better sense than to use a dog flea product on a cat unless it says on it, loud and clear, that it's safe to do so, but a cat can have a reaction even to a cat product, with foaming and drooling, trembling, or contracted pupils. He can even go into convulsions and coma. A swift and thorough bath should help, and if it doesn't, off to the vet.

At this writing, the oral flea killer Proban isn't licensed for cats in this country, though several other countries have okayed it. The Cat Hospital sometimes cautiously dispenses it in a crisis, but feels there must be some reason behind the hesitation.

There's an electronic flea collar on the market. It works on something called "pulsed, modulated, burst-circuit sound"; only a flea can hear it, and he hates it, and leaves. He can hear it up to four feet away, so he goes clear away and, presumably, starves. The collar runs on batteries, and it's entirely safe. The one available through The Sharper Image catalog is said to be twenty percent lighter and smaller than competing models, and thus more suitable for cats. It's expensive; if you have half a dozen cats it could run into major money, though perhaps if the cats spend a lot of time within four feet of each other one collar would do for all.

All proper books contain long lists of substances, from mothballs to marijuana, that can poison a cat, making the human dwelling sound like a feline deathtrap, but actually the Cat Hospital says it sees very few cases of poisoning. It's true there are plenty of things that could poison a cat if the cat ate them, but mostly the cat doesn't. What does happen is that something gets on the paws or the fur and the cat licks it off: whatever goes outside on a cat will get inside. Garden sprays and dusts, weed killers and insecticides are especially lethal, and we might ask the neighbors to let us know when they're going to be killing things in the vegetable patch or on the lawn so we can keep our cats indoors for a few days, or until it rains hard. And there may be spilled things in our own basements and garages, like engine oil or kerosene.

Poisoning is instant illness: the cat, well a few minutes ago, suddenly retches, slobbers, totters, and dilates or pinpoints its pupils. Unfortunately, it's hard to ask a cat what it ate. A half teaspoon of ipecac will make it vomit, or a teaspoon of hydrogen peroxide and water. (Many books suggest salt on the back of the tongue, but salt can have a toxic effect and is very strongly disrecommended by vets.) However, as with humans, we do *not* induce vomiting for petroleum-based products: paint, paint thinner or remover, kerosene, gasoline, benzene, fuel oil, floor wax, lighter fluid, or furniture polish. Or with corrosives like lye, washing soda, Drano, ammonia, metal polishes, or grease solvents. Or for strong acids or pine oil. For these, give milk or water.

If it might be insect repellents or the neighbors' garden poisons, carbon tetrachloride, or moth flakes, give water only, no milk.

For car anti-freeze, mysteriously appealing to cats, Sterno, and windshield de-icers, one source says vodka in milk is the treatment of choice.

If you spot the culprit on the paws or fur, plunge the cat into an immediate bath.

And, of course, you rush to the vet. Only, as with small children, these things happen with diabolical regularity on Sundays, late at night, or on Christmas morning, and finding the vet who's on emergency standby, or even rousing your own vet's answering service, can take a lifetime. A cat's lifetime. Those of us in the centers of civilization can at least hope that someone, somewhere, can be found to help. Country folk, though, should keep first-aid supplies on hand and fresh, remain alert, stay calm, think fast, and, when possible, drive like hell.

We should remember to think external for cat poisoning. To clean up spills. To lock cats away when disinfecting or polishing or painting or exterminating or dealing out death in the garden.

The list of poisonous plants is dismaying, and most lists make little distinction between leaves that kill at a glance and those that, if the cat eats the entire bush, roots and all, may give it a stomachache. Every Christmas we're warned that the whole festival is poisonous, the holly and the ivy, mistletoe, poinsettia, Christmas cherry, the works. (The tinsel on the tree is bad news too.) This year the little black cat ate some poinsettia to no ill effect; Dr. McDonough says it's really more an irritant than a poison. Mistletoe berries, though, fall readily on the floor and make intriguing toys, and we might just shuck them off before we hang the spray.

Bored cats indoors may take up plant eating for entertainment or, some say, because they need vegetables. Toss them a sprig of parsley or a carrot top and get rid of the ivy, the philodendron, and the avocado plant (which is probably dreary-looking anyway; they usually are). Replace with ferns. Cats and kittens that gleefully use the dirt in the pots as an in-house outhouse are sometimes discouraged by stockades of matches, toothpicks, or sharp sticks, and perhaps a mulch of stones.

Occasionally a vet will recommend a minute dosage of aspirin, but otherwise we may consider it cat poison; it hits their livers. If you drop one on the floor, or Tylenol, or ibuprofen, pick it up.

Pick everything up. More cats than get poisoned swallow, in an experimental way, unsuitable small objects. Threaded needles are lethally appealing. String in the intestine can be a killer, and rubber bands. The little black cat loves rubber bands, which appear all over this house without human agency; she hooks them over her lower teeth, pulls them down with her paw, and lets them go with a snap, a game so charming and harmless-looking that I feel like a monster snatching them away. Buttons. Paper clips. Safety pins. These otherwise adult creatures have no more sense than a two-year-old.

Open the mouth of a choking cat to see if you can see the problem and grab it with fingers or tweezers. If not, hold cat upside down and shake. If that doesn't help, try the Heimlich maneuver: holding cat upside down, pressed to your chest with your arms if you're alone, put a hand on each side of the chest and upper ribs and give a sharp squeeze. Get to the vet for help if possible. Even if the item goes clear on down, get to the vet; a small, smooth object might complete its journey, or it might not.

As with two-year-olds, when we see a cat playing with something, we go find out what it is.

Burns: Ice, cold compresses, or a twenty-minute cold bath.

Convulsions: Caused by various things, including simple stress. Just try to keep him from hurting himself, and if it lasts more than five minutes or he has another one within the hour, to the vet.

Heatstroke: Panting, weakness, staggering. Cool cat instantly with hose or basin of cold water, and think shame to have let it happen. Even with the windows open, a cat in a carrier can easily die in a hot car.

Wounds: Clip the hair from around it and clean with mild soap and water, no disinfectants. Abrasions and scratches usually heal by themselves, but bites and other punctures go to the vet, because they abscess. Actually, we often don't know they're there at all until they do.

Bleeding: Pressure bandage. If it bleeds through, hold it there and slap another on top. Tourniquets to be used only in darkest emergency and with great care, releasing frequently.

Broken legs: A dangling broken leg can be splinted with a pencil, table knife, squill of rolled paper, anything stiff and handy, to prevent tissue damage on the way to the vet. Tie it above and below the break, gently.

General injury: Wrap cat in towel or jacket or whatever and put it carefully in a box or slide in onto something stiff for carrying to the vet.

Electrical shock, from biting through lamp cords: Mouth-to-nose respiration. Close cat's mouth, take a breath, place your mouth over its nose and exhale very gently, then let the air back out. Proceed gently and slowly, ten to fifteen breaths per minute. Coat electrical cords with vinegar or Tabasco.

Diarrhea: Half a teaspoon Kaopectate after each trip to the box. If it persists or the cat seems otherwise ill, you can guess where to go next.

Constipation: A dab of Vaseline on the nose, to be licked off.

Hair balls: A splash of olive oil in the dinner.

Vitamins: From the vet, not the medicine cabinet, for pregnant and nursing mothers. Not to pop them in indiscriminately; too much is poisonous.

Other pills: When the vet says give him all of them, give him all of them. Resist the temptation known to us all to save out a few of those broad-spectrum antibiotics for an emergency, now that the cat is well again and howling for its dinner.

One popular book on cat care recommends regular doses of Valium for nervous or aggressive cats, but let's discuss it with our own vet first before sharing our tranqs around.

As the years begin to pile up on our cat, he may lose his relish for dinner. His teeth may need work. Probably they need cleaning. Or his sense of smell may be clouding over; he won't eat what he can't smell. A topping of something aromatic like tuna or sardines, or garlic if he likes it, may perk up his interest.

We should check him for tumors. Give him a thorough feel from time to time. Palpate the breasts, males as well as females, and most especially females unspayed or spayed late in life. Under the last pair toward the rear are two normal fatty pouches, but these feel smooth; what you're looking for feels nodular, like grape seeds. And check in his mouth for abnormal swellings or strange smells.

And make sure he can get up to his favorite places. Arrange steps and bridges. The view from the window is even more important in old age, and it's sad to jump and miss and be confined to the floor because no one's noticed you can't make it anymore.

Some say all cats should have their ears washed weekly

and be given thorough and regular baths. These, again, are the sterner sources, who may be recommending baths just to remind the cat who's boss around here. It seems to me a bath should be considered therapeutic intervention, for fleas, or poisons on the fur, or an accidental deluge of filth like the time Sidney went up the chimney, rather than routine hygiene.

A cat, after all, is a very workable item just as it comes from the package, and to feel that we should be constantly adjusting and tinkering with it to keep it in working order is hubris. It doesn't much need our advice on staying healthy. It's clean, it's sensible, and it doesn't drink or smoke. Its only really deplorable physical habit is a relentless passion for making kittens.

11

Sex and Kittens

Cats are famous for sex. Lion couples have been clocked at 120 matings in a day. All that sex, all those kittens, are rarely in the best interests of either the mother or the unwanted young, but what cat resists?

Although there are perhaps 56 million cats living under American roofs, there are somewhere between 15 and 25 million homeless, living hard, and the shelters kill over three million every year. It's irresponsible of the cats to keep adding to this tragedy, and irresponsible of us to let them.

"Neutering" is an unfortunate word. To neuter is to make neutral, to send to the sidelines, to make pale and wishy-washy, to negate, disarm, remove from the game. It sounds as if our bright, brisk cat were about to fade into a shadowy half-life more vegetable than animal. And even the most enlightened humans identify with this sexual obliteration, deep in their own organs, and shudder at murdering nature in their cats.

Men especially find castration hard to face, and when their loved Timmy or Charlie goes far afield in search of sex and gets killed by a car at the age of three, they console themselves with the natural, free life he led. They have lost their friend, and the cat has lost twelve or fifteen years of living, and the kittens he fathered probably led brief, desperate, and painful lives; the price is high.

There's also a widespread feeling that the neutered male turns fat and sleepy and becomes a blob of a cat, neutral indeed, but this isn't true. An intelligent cat will take up a number of peaceable, nonsexual pursuits and have time for all his hobbies; if he lives confined to an apartment and his hobby is food, he may indeed gain weight, but so would we all.

For the female, sex leads to what Don Marquis's Mehitabel called "just one damned kitten after another," but unspayed and unbred, her periods of fruitless yearning can lead, especially in the Siamese, to cystic ovaries and other female complications. They start young, too. At least one cat on record was pregnant when she was four months old. Between six and twelve months is more usual for the first heat. ("Heat" is considered vulgar, and nice people say "in season," like shad or asparagus, while scientific types say "in estrus" because it's always more delicate-minded to use words no one understands.) From then on her life, if unsupervised, consists of pregnancy, kittens, and pregnancy.

In truth, neutering is a wonderful release for a cat's life. Up till the age of sexual maturity a cat's world is wide and various and alive with rich experiences and discoveries and games and interesting things to do and ponder on; after maturity, all is sex. The sexual cat is like the human alcoholic or drug addict, its vision narrowed to a pinpoint, its mental landscape contracted to a single thought. The neutered cat expands again. Released from the blind all-absorbing monomania of making more cats, it can look around, rediscover human friendship, feline friendship, butterflies, scraps of paper, patches of sunshine, mice real and imaginary, humor, play. It's the neutered, not the "whole," cat that lives a full life exploring its potential. And of course it has more time for us; an unneutered tomcat is away on business a lot, and a producing female has little energy for human conversation.

All this said, and wicked as it is to add to the oversupply

of cats, fairness forces me to admit that a litter of kittens is by all odds the solidest entertainment value known to man. What can stage or screen offer that will keep us watching for weeks, cause us to neglect all else to watch, and make us laugh until the tears come, not just once but every evening for months? And all in the comfort of our own homes, all for the price of a little cat food.

And perhaps a stud fee. To be cynical, it helps to have purebreds when it's time to look for good homes. People who would turn up their noses at the most charming litter of blacks and grays and stripers will stand in line for our Persians or Siamese, and take good care of them too. People respect monetary value, and they like to think they're getting something valuable for nothing. The ordinary shorthair is not valuable, because of the aforementioned oversupply. It's common as dandelions, common as water, or bread, or sunlight, and any Tom, Dick, or Harry can have all he wants for the asking. When the neighbors' children come knocking with a carton full of kittens to give away, we are being pestered, not offered a gift beyond price. If the market could be cornered, if we could control the supply and pass restrictive ownership laws like the Egyptians', a litter of common kittens could make us richer than Whittington, but barring some disastrous epidemic it seems unlikely to happen.

The other advantage to purebred kittens is that you know roughly what you're going to get. The domestic shorthair, no matter how personally attractive, can surprise you with kittens God himself wouldn't adopt.

The female cat doesn't ovulate until copulation; copulation stimulates the ovaries to release the ova, which take up with any sperm they happen to meet. A cat can have kittens sired by two or three or more toms, each one more squincheyed, bowlegged, lanky, and particolored than the last. The lineup of patchwork pirates courting Betsy in the backyard spoke poorly for the futures of their offspring until the black cat showed up. He was partly Persian, fluffy, and round of eye and ear, all black and clearly a gentleman, dismayed by the bad language and scuffling among the competition; he seemed to have brought candy and flowers instead of brass knuckles. I invited him in. I locked him in the laundry room with Betsy for the night. In the morning I gave him breakfast, thanked him, and sent him home.

There were four kittens, three of them with "alley" stamped all over them. The fourth was Sidney. His whiskers were a curving waterfall of whisker, his round gold eyes were outlined with mascara, his nose was a sculpture of a nose, and all about him was shaped with generous grace. (Unfortunately, he was black and white in irregular patches, with a crooked black moustache, and ignorant people laughed and called him the Hitler Kitten. It takes cat people to see through the fur to the quality of cat beneath.)

From the way the female in heat carries on, you'd think any tom at all would do, but there does seem to be a certain selectivity at work, incomprehensible as it looks to us. Friends of mine had two cats, mother and daughter, who obliged the neighborhood toms by going into heat simultaneously, and obliged each other by babysitting their simultaneous litters. I was there when they were in heat, and a tom came to call. To the ignorant human eye he was immensely handsome, a most desirable father, a mackerel tabby with a dapper white bib and an ardent, anxious expression in his whiskers. They loathed him, mother and daughter. They exhausted their vocabulary of virginal distaste, these veterans of many litters. He clung to the windowsill, whimpering fondly, and they laid back their ears and hissed. Why? What were they looking for; what was wrong with this big, handsome lover? It's going much too far to suppose they sensed some genetic flaw in his ancestry. They rejected him; given a choice, female cats do choose.

Even the male can say no.

I thought about mating Morgan. Morgan thought about it too. Carl van Vechten refers to the female's "little amorous coos like the tender sighs of the eighteenth-century lover," but van Vechten wasn't thinking Siamese. When a Siamese female is calling for love the world hears, and it isn't exactly tender, either. Morgan called pleadingly for the first day or so, but then she lost patience completely and snarled with rage. She raced from window to window screaming threats like a fishwife, hoarsely furious with the absent unknown for his absence.

Hoping for kittens at least mostly Siamese, I tried to arrange things with my sister's blue-eyed Zachary. I put them in the basement together and closed the door. Morgan's screams made all the plumbing vibrate. Zachary tried to tear down the basement door to escape, and had left great splintery gashes in it by the time I let him out. He was almost two years old, but perhaps he wasn't ready. Science writer David Zimmerman believes that male cats, even when physically capable, need to mature socially and emotionally before they think about breeding, and Zachary's traumatic childhood and subsequent position as baby of the family may have retarded him. Or maybe the noise gave him a headache. Or maybe he was just rejecting Morgan. As soon as she calmed down, I had her spayed.

The feline penis has barbs on it, facing backward like the metal teeth guarding the gateways of parking lots, that may or may not influence ovulation. At the climax the female gives a piercing shriek and pulls away and slaps the tom. Some say this is because the barbs are painful, and some that this is just her way of showing pleasure; it isn't a point very likely to be resolved.

Infertility is not a feline problem: sex leads to kittens. For the good old domestic shorthair, gestation is from sixty-two to sixty-four days, while the Siamese takes longer, sixty-five to sixty-nine days. It's a good idea to check with a breeder before panicking about the various purebreds; gestation varies. We get a vitamin supplement from the vet, feed generously, and, toward the end, make a suitable kittening bed. She appreciates our thoughtfulness and likes to know the place is ready; some cats have even gone so far as to have their kittens in it. Bottom bureau drawers are often acceptable.

Many cats, even veterans, like encouragement and company in labor, and will follow us around talking about it, or wake us up to tell us. Abyssinians tend to get a bit hysterical, being Abyssinians. Some, even novices, take care of things alone. Blueberry woke me in the morning to show me her first and only litter, all clean and dry, in the box made ready for them. Sidney and his siblings were born on my bed, with me in it. Occasionally a worrying sort of cat will have them in a secret place of her own devising, often wildly unsuitable, like the clothes dryer or the pile of broken plaster behind the furnace or under the porch in bitter weather. When you finally discover them and move them to better quarters, she may keep on trying to hide them. Chippy was like that. Chippy hid kittens in boots and galoshes and under the attic floorboards and in the sleeves of my father's shirts in the laundry hamper. Her cleverest place was almost their last, far inside a roll of abandoned carpet in the basement, half smothered when we dragged them out. Chippy was striped: is this an aspect of what they mean when they say stripers are closest to the wild, that they don't entirely trust us with their young? Probably not; Chippy was always unstable.

If the cat has called on us to oversee the birth, usually all we need to offer is encouragement, kind words, and as much calm as we can muster. Once in a while there's trouble. When the kitten starts to come forth, whether front-end first or back, it should keep on coming. If it seems to have gotten stuck, clip your fingernails off short, wash your hands and grease them with Vaseline or butter or whatever's handy, and ease it slowly and gently out, holding the shoulders, not the head, and moving it out and downward from the mother's tail.

Kittens are born enclosed in a membrane like plastic wrap, and the mother's supposed to bite and lick this off their faces so they can breathe. If she seems confused and doesn't, break it yourself with your fingernails, swab the mucus out of the mouth, and perhaps give it a bit of a rub with a clean, soft cloth, all without moving it away from the mother. Watching you, she'll get the idea, and the kitten will mew for her, and she'll take over to finish the job.

She will eat the afterbirth. Don't recoil; this is important for hygienic and probably physiological reasons. She'll clean up the kittens and gather them to nurse, and purr. Bring her a snack and a bowl of water and tell her what a fine, brave cat she is. Replace the stained papers or old dish towels with something soft and go to bed. Quite likely in the morning you'll find one or two more kittens than you thought you had. They often pause in delivery like this; it's been suggested that in case some predator kills the first group, she'll have time to escape to a safer place and deliver another. Or it may just be that the double-lobed feline uterus empties itself one lobe at a time. Don't count your kittens before morning.

Sometimes there's a kitten refused. It may be the smallest and feeblest, or it may look perfectly all right to us but for some reason not to her. If it seems obviously sickly, maybe the best thing is just to let it slip away in its first hours, probably not suffering much, still deaf and blind, a marginal organism at best. If it looks healthy, we can have a try at changing her mind. Warm it with a hair dryer and a heating pad. Pick up a couple of the wanted kittens and mix them in our hands together with the unwanted one and then put them all back to feed; perhaps she won't be able to sort out the one she didn't want. If she still won't have it, and if we're enormously patient and stubborn, we can raise it as an orphan.

Sometimes something happens to the mother and we have a whole litter of orphans on our hands. And sometimes, cats being a queer bunch, she simply doesn't want her kittens at all. My sister's Mehitabel had her name before she had her kittens, but it was well chosen; she didn't like kittens. Maybe she'd been hoping for boys; she had no use for females. She refused to nurse them, and when people held her down and tried to feed her to them forcibly she hissed and slapped them, and wriggled free and ran away. When they peeped lonesomely for her, she left the house.

Judy raised them on an eyedropper, but Mehitabel can't stand them even now they're grown.

The original Mehitabel, Don Marquis's, observes cheerily that she has left her kittens in an abandoned garbage can where they will surely drown if it rains before she gets back.

Orphan kittens need the warmest place in the house, and a heating pad or a heat lamp. When their eyes start to open they need a dab of antibiotic ophthalmic ointment from the vet to take the place of maternal licking. They need help in defecating, a gentle massage with a warm, damp cotton swab or washcloth after each meal. They need our touching and handling. Most of all they need food, and they need it almost all the time. Pet stores carry a pet nurser, a specially designed plastic bottle more practical than the traditional eye-dropper. Pet stores or the vet can sell us Borden's KMR (Kitten Milk Replacer), which isn't cheap but it's carefully formulated to mimic mother's own and a lot less trouble than making the formula ourselves. If we can't get it, a standard recipe is a can of evaporated milk mixed with an equal amount of boiling water, an egg yolk, and a table-spoon of corn syrup or honey. Keep it refrigerated, and heat each meal before serving, maybe adding a single drop of human-infant vitamins for each kitten. Some experts say to feed them every four hours, but smaller meals every two hours seems safer. It's not a job to undertake lightly, and it's a hard one to abandon if we change our minds in mid-stream.

As they get older, they'll eat more and need it less often, like human babies, and eventually we'll be allowed to sleep all night again.

Happily, almost all cats make legendary good mothers. It's rare slow season for news that goes by without the paper printing a picture of a cat who has adopted and nursed a baby squirrel, puppy, rabbit, ferret, monkey, what have you. My grandmother had a cat named Keezo who adopted a small black chick, hatched in error to a Rhode Island

Red; the hen disowned it because it was the wrong color, but the cat didn't mind that it wasn't even a mammal.

Many are the stories of cats that have sacrificed their lives for their kittens. The theater cat in London, for instance, who had five kittens under the stage, and when the building burned carried four of them, one by one, to safety, and died struggling out with the fifth. (There's a worm at the heart of this story, as in the story of Ophelia's drowning reported in such close detail by Queen Gertrude's henchmen: why are you standing there taking notes, telling us what kinds of flowers she's holding, counting the desperate trips with kittens; isn't anyone going to *help*?)

Méry believes, and it seems reasonable, that the euphoric tenderness of the mother cat depends on her own security. A cat with a solicitous male in attendance, as in jaguar and some lion families, makes a joyful mother with playful young, while the tigress, who hasn't seen the male since mating, and the feral domestic cat makes anxious parents with fearful, precociously aggressive kittens. In human households kind people take the place of fathers, usually, though a resident father can be a careful parent too, and the mother, secure in room and board and safety, purrs so lavishly and takes such blatant pleasure in her young as to put the rest of us to shame. As they get older, she introduces them to the world and, sometimes with help from other cats around, educates them patiently.

With the usual exceptions, of course. There was a cat in my mother's childhood named Mrs. Johnson. Something was lacking in her chemical makeup, perhaps, since she was well past two before she produced her first litter, giving birth to four fine kittens on a pile of carrot-tops in the pantry. The kittens were particularly attractive, and she was a conscientious mother and housebroke them in a row of flowerpots on the porch. When they were at the peak of their charm, prancing around with their tails stuck up straight, she was seen leading them out of the backyard. They followed her in a neat line, like ducklings. She was heading for a patch of suburban woods between the house and the next street. About an hour later she came back alone. She ate, she washed, she hunkered down with her paws tucked in and closed her eyes, ignoring the family's shouted questions. Everyone fanned out and searched the neighborhood. They scoured the woods, they knocked on doors, they asked everyone. The kittens were old enough to scamper briskly and to squeal piercingly, but no one ever saw or heard them again, nor did their mother ever ask after them. She lived for many years after that and never had another litter.

Méry tells of a female who, when each successive litter was a week or so old, apparently tired of them and dropped them one by one through a balcony railing to their deaths on the tiles below.

Any instinctive passion as awesomely strong as the cat's for her kittens may sometimes, from the unwieldiness of its sheer power, tip itself over the edge in a few individuals, and turn inside out from love to murder. Even our own rational species isn't entirely above it, to judge from the tabloids.

In other times and places it was customary to drown the kittens at birth, so as not to become overburdened with cats, or, grudgingly, to "let her keep one." Softer-hearted modern Americans are more likely to keep them all for as long as they're young and cute, and then turn them out onto the streets at adolescence to fend for themselves. People like us, of course, bend every muscle to the task of having kind and responsible homes waiting for them when they're ready for homes. In the meantime, we have kittens, an occasion for rejoicing.

Until very recently the word was to leave young kittens strictly alone. Touching and handling them made them sickly and upset their mother, and the family children had to stand well back from the box and gaze from a distance. Now the powers that decide these things have decided otherwise, and the word is reversed: kittens should be handled. It speeds their development and promotes human friendship later in life. With the usual scientific precision, they tell us that each kitten should be handled for twenty minutes a day for the first thirty days, though it's unclear how they worked out this figure, and petting a blind, wriggling, screeching kitten for twenty minutes while its mother hovers anxiously could get tedious. With a litter of six it works out to a two-hour daily stint of kitten-touching, fourteen hours a week. It's well to remember that, through the decades when handling was forbidden, legions of cats developed normally and found human friendship; all revelations should be swallowed tentatively.

Anyway, even if we can't work the recommended schedule into our busy days, it's nice to know we're allowed to touch when we want to, though I've known mother cats who wouldn't have stood for it, not with newborns. If we'd tried it on Chippy's kittens she'd have hidden them for good and all. Discretion is advised.

Weaning is a cat's first major step into the wide world. As early as four weeks we can start offering them a saucer of evaporated milk and water mixed with some human baby meats and maybe a spoonful of baby rice flakes to give it body. They plunge their faces in it, sneeze and wade through it, dripping and bemused. Their mother may demonstrate by drinking it herself, and they may or may not bother to watch. Sometimes there's one leader kitten, brighter or more curious and vigorous than the rest, the first one to scramble out of the box, who gets the point right away, and one shy and tentative one who doesn't seem to care if he never learns. All go back to mother for dessert; it puts them to sleep, round-bellied and still making blissful sucking noises in their dreams.

The mother, seeing our willingness to fill saucers, encourages the process. Makes herself less available. Supervises. Leads them to the dish. (Sometimes a childless cat will take her toys in for supper and arrange them around the bowl, heads, if they have heads, pointing toward it.)

The help we offer is highly acceptable, but proper cats should learn to earn their living in a pinch, and a good mother will bring in mice if mice are available and show the kittens what to do with them. Some cats seem to have made the mental leap from hunting to husbandry that took humans so many millennia: they start mouse farms, to ensure a steady supply. A friend of mine had a cat who kept mice in the bathtub, readily available and trapped by the slippery sides. One writer claims that his Siamese stored mice in his grand piano, and when the kittens grew up and went away she lost interest in the mice, being a good mother but not a serious hunter, and the unused supplies flourished and multiplied and made merry in the workings of the piano for years.

There's a lot to the education of a kitten, and it's best to leave them with their mothers for as long as possible, nine weeks at least. Unfortunately, weaning time, six weeks or so, is often considered departure time, since the mother's owners are understandably anxious not to get stuck with kittens far advanced in gangly adolescence. But there's so much we can't teach them; who knows how much? A friend insists that his mother cat spoke to her kittens for fifteen minutes every morning. It wasn't scolding, he says; it sounded like an instructive lecture, and the kittens paid close attention. No one can guess what she told them, but their various later owners all swore they grew up to be the finest and smartest cats in the entire state of Georgia.

Aside from us primates, only cats have been tested and proven to learn from watching others, and tree climbing is definitely a case in point. Going up is instinctive; getting down is not, as many a cat-owner has learned. The kitten goes up gaily, gets to the first branch, or the fifth or sixth if it's brave and reckless, and sits on it and screams for help. Then its mother or another cat will climb up to it and demonstrate "down," backwards, to take advantage of the hooked claws, and looking over the shoulder like a rower until it's close enough to jump. Sometimes the kitten is too busy screaming to pay attention, and I've watched an unrelated adult male climb and unclimb a tree three times, infinitely patient, before the kitten understood.

If we insist on keeping the kittens until their education is complete, we have that much more time to watch kittens. This is entertainment of a high order, witty, charming, and sophisticated; comic routines refined for thousands of years, dancing Geminis of stagecraft, masters and mistresses of the "Oops, where did I put it? Oh, there it is!" spin, vertical leap of pretended astonishment, king-of-the-mountain, mistaken identity, dance to inaudible pipers, and the quick over-the-shoulder glance; are you watching? are you laughing, am I charming enough, shall I have a home? Kittens play, of course; kittens play when no one is watching, but no regular audience can doubt that some of this is for us. We're being courted as well as entertained. Watch me, watch me hide and spring out on my sister, pretend to be frightened, dance onto my hind legs with my eyes wide and my paws outstretched: can you resist? If it's agreed, then we can put some of this aside. Sign here, and we will be free to become a cat. It's the way it's always been.

Step by step they learn the lessons in etiquette, communication, hunting, hygiene, competition, cooperation, and friendship necessary for their lives, and frolic to charm their way into homes, and begin to change from kittens into cats.

Kittens are not cats; kittens are hardly even similar to cats, any more than caterpillars are to moths. There's a change that takes place, if you're watching, toward the end of the first year, that has nothing to do with sexual maturity. The kitten deepens, and takes on the resonance and shadow of a cat. Cats go on playing, they play all their lives, but we're no longer being asked to laugh. We aren't being courted. The relationship has changed, and if we've taken the time to be a figure in its life, it will want something more from us, confident in its home and focusing on us now as complete and separate beings. It wants our friendship now, a friendship between very different equals, and even something more than friendship, for reasons neither we nor it will ever really understand.

12

Practical Cats

Allergies, human: Bulletin boards are laden with notices trying to give away cats because someone's allergic. In the Cat Hospital, a sad letter was posted by a young woman about to get married, looking for a home for a cat she clearly loved, a cat in middle age, a cat no one was going to want; her intended was allergic to it. People passing through the waiting room had added comments on its margins: "Don't marry him!!!" "You'll be sorry," and "Bad trade!"

My next-door neighbor loves cats, and always stops to converse with mine when they sit on the windowsill supervising the street. She had always had cats. Alas, her husband is allergic to them, and all she can do now is chat with Morgan through the screen.

My son brought home a kitten, and his girlfriend sneezed and sneezed and her eyes watered, and now the kitten lives with me instead.

In a book I found a recipe for allergy-proofing cats, involving a coat conditioner and a bath in a solution of Downy fabric softener, and asked Dr. McDonough about it; she thought the Downy solution was far too strong but that, suitably watered down, it was worth a try. She said sometimes she recommended wiping the cat down with the fabric-softener sheets designed to go in the dryer. Then I read about Dust Seal.

Dust Seal was developed initially for people whose rugs and curtains make them sneeze, but after investigation it was pronounced harmless for use on animals. I sent for some. It arrived promptly and proved to be an innocuous, odorless white gruel, the consistency of Spackle mixed on the wet side. Stir a tablespoonful into a pint of water and sponge cat with it. I tried it on Barney as being the most allergenic-*looking* of them all; I know it isn't the fur itself, it's the dander, and length of coat doesn't count, but the very sight of all that puffball fur makes some people sneeze. To his annoyance, I sponged him down thoroughly and sent him off to spend a week in a small apartment with my son's girlfriend.

He was homesick, but she was fine.

According to the accompanying literature, once a month is often enough to rinse the cat (or dog, or rabbit, or horse; a horse might run into money). Fifteen dollars plus postage buys what looks like enough for a year or two, at least, since the pint of the recipe makes more than enough for even a Persian, and it comes by mail from Willner Chemists, 330 Lexington Avenue, New York, NY 10157, or direct from the makers, L.S. Green Associates, 162 West 56th Street, New York, NY 10019.

Of course, there's the strong possibility that "allergic" is a euphemism, a polite way to tell a cat person that one hates cats, finds them sneaky, sinister, and untrustworthy, and has recurring nightmares about finding them in one's bed, briefcase, shoes, etc.

In these cases it's doubtful that Dust Seal will help, and you might have to consider finding a good home for the person in question.

Bathtubs: They make good playpens. Ping-Pong balls, for instance, are splendid cat toys but have a habit of finding their way under the furniture, out of reach. A nice thing to do for a housebound cat is to put a couple in the bathtub where they can't escape and make a satisfying billiards sort of noise against the sides.

Catnip: A member of the mint family, catnip is hardy and easy to grow and hard to synthesize; most "catnip" toys you buy contain only wood chips sprayed with a chemical substance supposed, by humans, to smell like catnip, though not very much like catnip.

The plant is easy to grow in any waste corner of the yard that gets some sun and isn't soggy; it will grow in a deep pot on a sunny fire escape or patio or balcony. The only problem is protecting it from its fans.

In 1774 Goldsmith's *Natural History* stated, "The cat . . . is excessively fond of some plants such as valerian, marum, and cat-mint; against these it rubs, and smells them at a distance, and at last wears them out." Cats have no agricultural restraint; carnivores live for the moment. Plant a nice stand of catnip, and as soon as it rears its little heads the nearest cat will bite them off at ground level and then roll in the remains to make a scented dust bowl.

Catnip seeds can be had from most seed catalogs, listed under herbs. Start them according to directions in a safe place: a sunny windowsill in a room you can close against cats, or a spot on the far side of a closed door or window. When started in or transplanted to the open world they need a cage. A strong cage. I tried chicken wire first, but the cats just leaned against it until it collapsed. Sturdy metal stakes or cages such as garden centers sell to support tomatoes would be fine. I was lucky to find part of a rusty roll of sheep fencing, and Sidney, cat of infinite patience, sat beside it all summer as if at a mousehole waiting for the sprigs to grow through to him.

In June and again before hard frost, harvest it by cutting it back halfway, and bring the results inside to a dry, airy place away from direct sun. Tie the stalks together in bunches and hang them head down, well out of cat reach, until the leaves are dry enough to crumble in your fingers. Lock the cats in another room and strip it onto newspapers, discarding the tough stems. The hard black specks that sink to the bottom are seeds, if you want to increase your holdings. The more catnip you grow the less the cats will bother it, being jaded with plenty and content all summer with an occasional nibble; by snowfall they'll be avid again.

Store the dried catnip in a plastic bag in refrigerator, freezer, or bank vault; don't suppose for a minute that the cat can't sniff it out through a plastic bag, or twenty plastic bags and a cupboard door. Dole it out sparingly. A pinch on the rug goes a long way and leaves the rug desirable for days.

When you have a surplus you use it as a Christmas present for other cat owners. For a while there I made it up into proper felt mice with yarn tails and whiskers, and then I degenerated into felt bags tied with ribbons, and now, being pressured for leisure, I hand it over in a sandwich bag; no cat cares about the container. It makes a more original party gift than the usual bottle of wine, and besides, it's free. Some few people object to it on moral grounds, especially those who reveled in recreational drugs in their youth and repented, but everyone knows cats have no morals.

No one seems to know exactly why catnip pleases cats. Chemists say the compound that does it is cis-transnepetatalactone, which doesn't clear things up much. Apparently circus trainers were the first to use it, dosing their lions, who dropped instantly into besotted docility. Lions must react differently; my cats chase each other in circles, knock over lamps, speak in tongues, and pile the rugs up in corners. I'd hate to be in a cage with a lion that felt that way.

The United States government, it grieves me to report, has been known to use catnip to lure bobcats and pumas to their deaths.

Most veterinarians approve of it as a tonic, antidepressant, and stress reducer, but some of the puritanical sources, bothered by the thought of cats having fun, refer to it sniffily as a "stimulant" and caution against offering it frequently, which is silly because its effects diminish quickly with overuse. If it's a drug, it's self-limiting; unlike the things humans play with, the more they have the less they want. For maximum effect, ration strictly.

You can steep yourself a tea of it and try it as a cure for colds, nervous headaches, and insomnia, but it won't make you feel the way the cats feel. Pity. We could use something like that, along about February.

So can the cats.

It's considerate little touches like a cushion on a sunny windowsill and a supply of home-grown catnip that make *Felis* glad to be *domesticus*, and satisfied to keep us company.

Diseases, human: There isn't much except fleas that people can catch from cats, but there is toxoplasmosis.

Although more human cases of toxoplasmosis come from eating undercooked meat or digging bare-handed in the garden, it's possible to get it from cats. It's caused by a parasite, and threatening mainly to unborn children as a cause of birth defects, so some cool-hearted doctors simply advise pregnant woman to throw their cats away. This isn't necessary, and if your cat never gets raw meat and doesn't go outdoors or eat mice there's very little chance it could be infected. Still, there are some simple precautions to take. The parasite passes through the cat and into the litter box, where it has to ripen and mature for several days before it turns dangerous; obviously, if you take the feces out of the box every day you never get any ripe parasites. (I'm told that many doctors insist on having the husband or other nonpregnant family members clean the litter box, but this has resulted in blameless cats being taken to shelters or turned from their doors to starve.) Use a scoop to lift the feces out and flush it down the toilet. Wear gloves when gardening. Wash hands after dealing with raw meat. Don't eat raw meat or feed it to your cat.

The vet can test the cat to see whether it's been exposed and the doctor can test the woman to see if she has; like measles, it doesn't strike twice, and a pregnant woman previously exposed to toxoplasmosis has nothing to worry about.

I understand we expect a vaccine, to be given to the cat, not the person, but it isn't on the market yet. In the meantime, refrain from panic and keep the litter box clean.

Eye contact: A cat likes to look at you, and likes you to look at him. Simply patting him while trying to read the paper isn't good enough; you have to look. Looking is conversation for cats, and even the youngest kitten, as soon as it can focus, will look you straight in the eye from ankle level. Some cats, when feeling especially fond of you, slowly close their eyes, like blowing a kiss. It's polite to answer. Close your own eyes back at him, slowly. Because a cat feels pleasant to the hand, we rely too much on the crudities of physical contact, but, as the Egyptians knew, eyes matter in cats, eyes are their signature, and seeing is their deft and elegant touch on their friends. The hand without the eye is an empty message to send back.

Fur on clothes: A roll of Scotch tape, carried at all times, is useful for quick touch-ups before attending business meetings and dinner parties. Wrap a loop of it sticky-side-up around your fingers and dab.

Games: There are various games a human can play with a cat, such as trailing a piece of string or accidentally moving the toes under the blanket, and various games a cat can play with a human, such as making him throw things to be retrieved. I don't know if it's possible, or desirable, to teach this to a cat, but some seem to come by it naturally. Charlie retrieved crumpled cigarette packs, but only my brand, Pall Malls. He even retrieved them after they'd been put in the trash and covered with coffee grounds and eggshells. Guests thought it was cute, and encouraged him, and kept throwing his cigarette pack across the room all evening, and he kept on bringing it back, and the guests left with pitcher's elbow. It was a repetitious, unimaginative game more suited to dog than cat, but Charlie was an unimaginative cat.

Then my husband and I quit smoking. Charlie sulked, and languished, until one day my husband came to me and accused me of cheating; Charlie had just brought him a crumbled Pall Mall pack. Later, when I let him out into the courtyard between the apartment buildings, as was our custom, he vanished into the area where the trash cans were kept. Ten minutes later he bounded back triumphant with a crumbled Pall Mall pack in his jaws; somebody out there smoked our brand. I suppose it was the only kind appropriate for retrieving; I suppose they smell distinctive. The game went on. And on, and on.

Hot weather: When traveling with a cat on a hot day, put a plastic bag full of ice cubes in the carrier. Keep noticing how the sun slants in through the car windows as you drive and try to keep the case away from it. Black carriers are particularly lethal, soaking up heat. If you park in the shade when you stop for lunch, remember the sun moves; leafy shade at noon may be red-hot broiler by one. Get a carrier with maximum air flow. If in spite of all your cat starts staggering from the heat, cool it off instantly with all the water available.

In China: A special breed of long-haired cat is raised for its meat, and forms one of the essential ingredients in the classic Dragon-Tiger-Phoenix dish, representing the tiger. The dragon is usually snake, they say, and in the absence of phoenixes their part is supplied by the humble chicken. I don't have the exact recipe.

Jumping: Just because none of our previous cats has ever been able to jump up onto something or down from somewhere doesn't mean that nobody can. Some are better athletes than others, or braver, or sillier. Never assume that the new kitten, when it gets a bit more growth on it, can't jump from the balcony into the street below, or up from the deck onto the neighbors' roof.

Some vets warn us to prevent pregnant cats from high jumping. They don't say how.

Kittens, choosing: They tell us that if we have a litter to choose from, to pick the number-two kitten. Not the first one out of the box, the bravest and most curious, because, they say, it's likely to make trouble. And not the independent one who doesn't hang out with the others and goes off on its own, because it may not want to socialize with us, either. And while sympathy is a virtue, not the one that huddles sadly in a corner with its coat rough and its eyes running.

Advice is useless; kittens get chosen for unscientific reasons like suddenly crawling into our laps and purring. When I went to pick a Siamese kitten, one of them, bored with being inspected, decided to leave the room and I tried to detain him by his little spike of a tail, and he whirled around with a preposterous great shout of outraged dignity; he's still shouting, Corvo is, and when he asks for a lap the glassware trembles.

Litter pans: There's an amazing variety of products available for deodorizing litter pans; things to spray on top of the mess or stir in with it or spread out under it, and disinfectants to wash the pan with and plastic houses to contain it and its noxious smell. Changing the litter seems to be a kind of last resort, to try only when all else fails.

If there's a dead horse in your back yard, you don't keep spraying it with aerosol cans of Piney Woods or Strawberry Fields, you have the horse removed.

Cat litter is a great nuisance. It's heavy, heavy to buy and carry home and even heavier to drag out with the trash. People quite naturally strive to have each ten-pound bag last as long as possible, and longer. After a while it smells.

Cats are sensitive about their toilet functions, and have sensitive noses. If the pan smells bad to us, it must be agony to a cat, and going into one of those plastic litter-houses something like walking into the jaws of hell. A cat outdoors covers up its droppings and then turns to sniff the area to make quite sure no other creature can tell what happened there. A litter pan that tells the world what happened must be a worry, and a cat will keep trying to erase the smell, scratching the floor around it, trying to pull the shower curtain down over it.

On the other hand, what the manufacturer says smells like Strawberry Fields smells to a cat of mysterious and probably threatening chemicals, the predators of outer space, Dobermans from Mars.

All in all, it's good of them to use a litter pan at all.

People who work professionally with problem cats say that nine out of ten cases of cats "breaking training," as they say (rather like a football player sneaking a cigarette), can be traced to pan conditions.

We must take up the burden of cat-keeping and carry it, home from the store, out for the trash. No chemicals. No roofs, no disinfectants, no scented sprays. Just fresh litter, and a little plain water to rinse the pan, or use a plastic liner. And instead of using twice as much as recommended, hoping to make it last four times as long, use half as much, to last half as long.

A handful of baking soda mixed with the litter does no harm, and some swear by a handful of 20 Mule Team Borax. But there's no substitute for a fresh start.

Moving: A lot of cats vanish during the chaos of moving. It's heavy stress for a cat, even more so than for us since the motives are inexplicable, and home is a deeply personal matter to a cat; to have great shouting strangers burst in and start manhandling his furniture must be a nightmare.

Put the cat in his carrier before the movers come, and put the carrier in the quietest place, the car if possible, parked in a cool spot, or the bathroom. Leave him in the carrier. Take him to the new quarters and put the carrier in the quietest place or leave it in the car. Don't let him out until the movers have been paid off and gone away and the door is firmly shut. Even then, it's sensible to turn him loose gradually; this is a profoundly shaken cat, and may be happier locked in a bedroom with a bowl of water and some used and personally scented clothing of your own thrown around. Even if it's a safe area for a cat to go outdoors, best to keep him in the house for a week or two to get his bearings and calm down. Get acquainted with the resident spirits and hallucinations before he has to deal with the territory problem. Spoil him a little. You can even butter his paws, if he likes butter.

Novelty: The more businesslike books on cat care feel that a cat's needs are entirely nutritional and medical, and once he's properly fed and vetted your responsibilities are over. Routine, they say, is soothing to a cat, and he resents change; feed him at the same hour every day and he will be content.

I don't know. I suppose some cats resent change, maybe an old and crotchety cat whose favorite sofa has been sold down the river, but a predator's natural life is pretty various. No two days are alike, and no two meals arrive in the same way, let alone at the same hour, and the scents of his surroundings change with every breeze. Grazing animals enjoy monotony, and in the unvaried routine of a zoo a zebra will stand broadside to the same sunlight in the same enclosure, his lower lip twitching with pleasure, every day for ten years, but the panther paces back and forth.

I think a cat in confinement needs as much novelty as we can arrange. Even in the city, a cat can be taken out in a safe figure-eight harness, can go to the park if he's not afraid of passing dogs. A view of a busy street and pigeons helps. An occasional dose of catnip, change of diet, new place to sit, new cat in the household, a visit to a neighbor's apartment, a canary in a cage to lust for, a wind-up toy, human guests. Something to think about. Cats are intelligent, however strangely their intelligence works, and how can an intelligent creature keep its mind awake contemplating the same walls and smelling the same smells for years without change?

Opening doors: Where cats go out, opening doors to let them out and back in again has been a source of irritation and marital discord ever since cats moved in with us. Cat doors can be made in human doors, through which the cat may come and go without having to wake up the whole household. Sometimes the cat will invite friends in. In the country, it's not unheard of for the householder to go downstairs in the night investigating strange sounds and trip over a skunk in the dark kitchen.

There are cat doors on the market that are opened by a magnet on the cat's collar, activating a solenoid that releases the catch on the door to admit your cat, and only your cat. I don't know why they don't extend the idea to people and people doors, eliminating the need for door keys.

Pussywillows: A long time ago in Poland, an unwanted litter of kittens was thrown in the river to drown. Their mother sat on the bank and wept so long and so bitterly for them that the willows growing along the river's edge took pity on her and held down their branches for the drowning kittens to cling to. After that, every spring the willow bushes have sprouted soft little velvet buds like kittens' paws.

Qualyway: In Cornwall, this will cure a sty:

Take the tail of a black cat and stroke your eye outward from the nose, giving one stroke to each phrase as you chant:

> *I poke thee,*
> *I don't poke thee,*
> *I toke the quell that's under the eye.*
> *Oh, qualyway.*
> *Oh, qualyway.*

Renting: In the United States, and only in the United States, land of the free, it's the rule rather than the exception for landlords and rental agents to make as much fuss over a house cat on the premeses as if one were harboring a brothel, or a rock band. No one seems to know why we put up with this, or why it happens in the first place, unless Americans came so recently to a wild country that we distrust all animals as the opposite of civilization, as unpredictable, probably dangerous, certainly unclean.

In Soviet Russia, home of oppression and the trampling of human rights, everyone, no matter how cramped the apartment, has cats and dogs, though some of the newer buildings try to limit the number of dogs to three, and the government provides free veterinary care.

In America, cats make criminals of decent folk. Me, for instance. For my rented house I signed a lease swearing to have no pet of any kind, not even a caged bird, nor to let any sort of creature pass through or inhabit the premises no matter how briefly. I am careful to pay my rent promptly, to deal with and pay for all repairs myself, and to keep my fingers crossed. I can be thrown out onto the street without further ado if I'm discovered. There is no legal recourse. My landlord is under no obligation to prove damage or cite complaints. He holds a month's rent of mine as guarantee that I and mine will do no more than ordinary damage, but apparently the potential for feline destruction is more than that would cover.

Every rental agent makes his own rules, and I once had a most generous lease that allowed me to own as many as two cats or dogs that weighed no more than twenty pounds, but most stand firm against all creatures.

I read a letter from a woman who waited five years for a public housing unit, and when she finally got it was told she could have only one cat. She managed to find homes for the other two, and then was told she had to take out a twenty-thousand-dollar insurance policy against her remaining cat's killing or injuring anyone.

Countless once-loved cats are gassed in the shelters because of landlords. Countless lonely, law-abiding citizens live without companions because of them. Convalescents, the depressed, and the elderly, needing the medical benefits of pet therapy, go without it. It's a mystery impenetrable that pets are not subject to the logic of leases, that no one will wait till the damage is done and claim payment for it, no one will wait till the neighbors complain and then evict the cat, no one will wait till it does kill someone and then demand restitution; it's taken for granted ahead of time that pets will destroy the property, cause bodily injury, and enrage the neighborhood; they are guilty before the crime is committed by reason of being themselves.

Even more mysterious is why we, alone of the world's peoples, put up with it.

Stains & spots: A cat that wolfs its dinner often throws it up again almost immediately, unchanged. Rarely on the kitchen tiles, rarely on the bare floor, usually on rugs and upholstery. No matter how promptly it's cleaned up, it leaves a pinkish-brown stain. This is from the dyes added to the cat food to make it more appealing, more meat-like, to the human eye. Most of the scientific, non-supermarket cat foods are made without dyes, a good idea for vomiters. In the meantime, after wiping it up, wash the area with a dab of dish soap and douse it with club soda, which takes out the dye stains and odors. White vinegar works too.

A cat that has used the rug for toilet purposes may go back and use the same place again. After applying one of the above, cover the area with double-sided sticky tape, most disagreeable to the paws, until the matter has been forgotten.

Traps, household: Cats are always getting closed into things. It's the nature of the cat to get into closable places, private, secret places like cupboards and closets and clothes dryers, bureau drawers and garden sheds and furnace rooms. Being well down below eye level, they get locked in unseen.

Before combing the neighborhood and posting frantic signs offering a large reward, open everything closable.

Before turning on the washing machine, dryer, or even the oven, feel around inside.

Up or underneath: There's a basic psychological difference between the wary cat posted on high ground, on strategic vantage points like a bookshelf or a tree, and the cat squeezed underneath something and trembling in its farthest corner. Up is a good place to be; you can see farther, and you can leap down on the enemy, and you're safe from dogs. Up is sensible; under is stark terror, and the hope of being unseen by an enemy against whom you have no recourse. A cat checking out its territory goes up, a cat in a hostile new household goes under.

This observation does not apply to the cat under the bed, who knows full well how hard it is for humans to rout out and hopes to be left there until the people have gone to sleep so it can emerge and snuggle under the covers.

Variety: *See* Novelty, above.

Walking with cats: Country cats like to go for a walk with their people. Do not invite a cat to walk with you if you have a time limit, or even a purpose. Cats walk more slowly than people. Cats, except at dinnertime, do not think in terms of destination. And cats refuse to hurry when urged to and resent being scooped up and carried. If you've gone too far, they complain bitterly. A country walk with a cat should include various rocks, benches, or fallen trees where the human can sit and wait until the cat is ready to proceed.

People who want to sell us leashes and harnesses for walking city cats illustrate their ads with cats striding briskly along the sidewalk beside their owners. The truth is, a harnessed cat is no more goal-oriented than a loose cat, and the complex instructions for training your cat to walk down the street like a person are fairy tales; walking from point A merely to get to point B is not a catly concept. We can, however, harness and leash the cat and carry it to a quiet spot or vacant lot or park and let it poke around and smell the interesting smells. We follow it where it wants to go, unwinding the leash from obstacles. A cat outside on the common ground of a city is on very strange territory, territory not its own, land already claimed by total strangers, mostly dogs; it would be an insensitive cat indeed who could simply march through this alien wilderness like a man on his way to the bus stop.

When we get bored with standing around, we pick it up and carry it home again. "Walk" is the wrong word.

Extra cats: They go to the shelters to be gassed. Not out onto the streets to starve or be killed in traffic. Not out to the country to be pushed from the car in some wooded spot where, we tell ourselves, there must be plenty of mice. Not to be pressed on friends who genuinely don't want them. To the shelters. The shelters won't be surprised to see us; they kill millions every year.

Yowling: According to the surviving cartoons, it used to be the custom to throw shoes. I suppose shoes were the handiest heavy object in a dark bedroom, and perhaps they used to be cheaper than they are now. It's unlikely that a sleepy human pitching his footwear at a sound somewhere out in the darkness ever actually hit a cat, or stopped the yowling if he did.

We can stop our own from yowling by having them altered, but little can be done about those alone in the world.

Zero population growth: A goal to strive for. *See* Extra Cats, above.

When Chateaubriand was French ambassador in Rome, Pope Leo XII, near death, presented him with his own dear cat Micetto. Later Chateaubriand wrote to Mme. Recamier, "I have as companion a big greyish-red cat with black stripes across it. It was born in the Vatican, in the Raphael loggia. Leo XII brought it up in a fold of his robes where I had often looked at it enviously when the Pope gave me an audience . . . I am trying to make it forget exile, the Sistine Chapel, the sun on Michelangelo's cupola, where it used to walk, far above the earth."